"This book offers a passionate and persuasive case for using arts-based research methods in educational research. Filled with many different practical examples, it shows how arts-based methods extend the repertoire of research approaches and open new research routes for attending to relationships, affects, bodies, and language. In showing how arts-based methods help promote rigour in research, contribute to decolonising knowledge, shift hierarchies of knowledge-power relations, and inform policy making, it makes an important argument for arts-based methods as a form of research activism".

Carol A. Taylor, *Professor of Higher Education and Gender, University of Bath, UK*

"Based on the author's 'hands-on' experience, this book provides a much-needed, accessible text on the power and possibilities of arts-based methods. It explores their transformative potential and how they can facilitate the agency of research participants and reframe power relationships. Whilst shining a light on the value of arts-based methods, Dr Tian does not shy away from exploring controversies and risks that researchers need to be aware of in using these methods. The result is an invaluable text for those new to and for those experienced in arts-based methods".

Philip A. Woods, *Professor of Educational Policy, Democracy and Leadership, University of Hertfordshire, UK*

"Exactly the kind of critically oriented, unique, and insightful book that set the stage for Art-based Research Methods for Educational Researchers grounded on enriching articulation of both ontology, epistemology, and vast research close-to-practice in using this methodology as a form of advocacy and activism. This deep, comprehensive, solid, and thorough foundational book is highly recommended for instructors, postgraduate students, and practitioners alike for a deeper understanding and use of art-based educational research".

Khalid Arar, *Professor of Education and Community Leadership, Texas State University, USA*

Arts-Based Research Methods for Educational Researchers

Arts-Based Research Methods for Educational Researchers is a book for early-career and established scholars who aim to use the arts to spark new ideas and empower participants in educational research. It will allow readers to conduct arts-based research in their own projects.

The book starts with a brief history of the arts in research, going on to provide an in-depth understanding of the philosophical foundations of arts-based research—different research designs, material preparation, ethical considerations, data collection, analysis, and reporting. Chapters highlight the impact of arts-based research, how it can be used to facilitate positive changes in educational research, practice, and policymaking. Tian suggests avenues for those who want to further develop these methods, guiding readers to reflect on their positionality and ethical issues involved in the research process.

This insightful book is ideal for early career and experienced educational researchers who use qualitative methods in their inquiries. It offers a reader-friendly guide to methodology for scholars, educators as well as undergraduate and postgraduate students.

Dr Meng Tian is Associate Professor of Educational Leadership at the University of Birmingham, UK. Her interest lies in applying innovative research methods to study complex leadership, power, and social justice issues in education.

Qualitative and Visual Methodologies in Educational Research
Series Editors: Rita Chawla-Duggan and Simon Hayhoe
University of Bath, UK

We are increasingly living in an era where students and researchers are under severe time pressures, whilst the amount of research topics, methodologies, data collection methods, and ethical questions continue to grow. The *Qualitative and Visual Methodologies in Educational Research* series provides concise, accessible texts that take account of the methodological issues that emerge out of researching educational issues. They are ideal reading for all those designing and implementing unfamiliar qualitative research methods, from undergraduates to the most experienced researchers.

Books in the series:

- Are compact, comprehensive works, to appeal to final year undergraduates and early career postgraduates, at masters and doctoral level—both PhD and EdD. These works can also be easily read and digested by emerging, early career researchers, or raise issues applicable to experienced researchers who are keeping up with their field.
- Reflect on a single methodological problem per volume. In particular, the titles examine data analysis, research design, access, sampling, ethics, the role of theory, and how fieldwork is experienced in real-time.
- Have chapters that discuss the context of education, teaching, and learning, and so can include a psychological as well as social and cultural understanding of teaching and learning in non-traditional or non-formal, as well as formal settings.
- Include discussions that engage critically with ontological and epistemological debates underpinning the choice of qualitative or visual methodologies in educational research.

The *Qualitative and Visual Methodologies in Educational Research* series includes books which stimulate ideas and help the reader design important and insightful research that improves the lives of others though education, to ultimately inspire the development of qualitative and visual methodologies.

Titles in the series include:

Emancipatory and Participatory Research for Emerging Educational Researchers
Theory and Case Studies of Research in Disabled Communities
Joe Barton and Simon Hayhoe

Arts-Based Research Methods for Educational Researchers
Meng Tian

For more information about this series, please visit: www.routledge.com

Arts-Based Research Methods for Educational Researchers

Meng Tian

LONDON AND NEW YORK

First published 2023
by Routledge
4 Park Square, Milton Park, Abingdon, Oxon OX14 4RN

and by Routledge
605 Third Avenue, New York, NY 10158

Routledge is an imprint of the Taylor & Francis Group, an informa business

© 2023 Meng Tian

The right of Meng Tian to be identified as author of this work has been asserted in accordance with sections 77 and 78 of the Copyright, Designs and Patents Act 1988.

All rights reserved. No part of this book may be reprinted or reproduced or utilised in any form or by any electronic, mechanical, or other means, now known or hereafter invented, including photocopying and recording, or in any information storage or retrieval system, without permission in writing from the publishers.

Trademark notice: Product or corporate names may be trademarks or registered trademarks, and are used only for identification and explanation without intent to infringe.

British Library Cataloguing-in-Publication Data
A catalogue record for this book is available from the British Library

Library of Congress Cataloging-in-Publication Data
Names: Tian, Meng, 1984– author.
Title: Arts-based research methods for educational researchers / Meng Tian.
Description: First Edition. | New York : Routledge, 2023. | Series: Qualitative and visual methodologies in educational research | Includes bibliographical references and index.
Identifiers: LCCN 2022055576 (print) | LCCN 2022055577 (ebook) | ISBN 9781032051222 (Hardback) | ISBN 9781032051239 (Paperback) | ISBN 9781003196105 (eBook)
Subjects: LCSH: Education—Research—Methodology. | Art in education—Philosophy. | Qualitative research—Methodology.
Classification: LCC LB1028 .T49 2023 (print) | LCC LB1028 (ebook) | DDC 370.72/1—dc23/eng/20221129
LC record available at https://lccn.loc.gov/2022055576
LC ebook record available at https://lccn.loc.gov/2022055577

ISBN: 978-1-032-05122-2 (hbk)
ISBN: 978-1-032-05123-9 (pbk)
ISBN: 978-1-003-19610-5 (ebk)

DOI: 10.4324/9781003196105

Typeset in Times New Roman
by Apex CoVantage. LLC

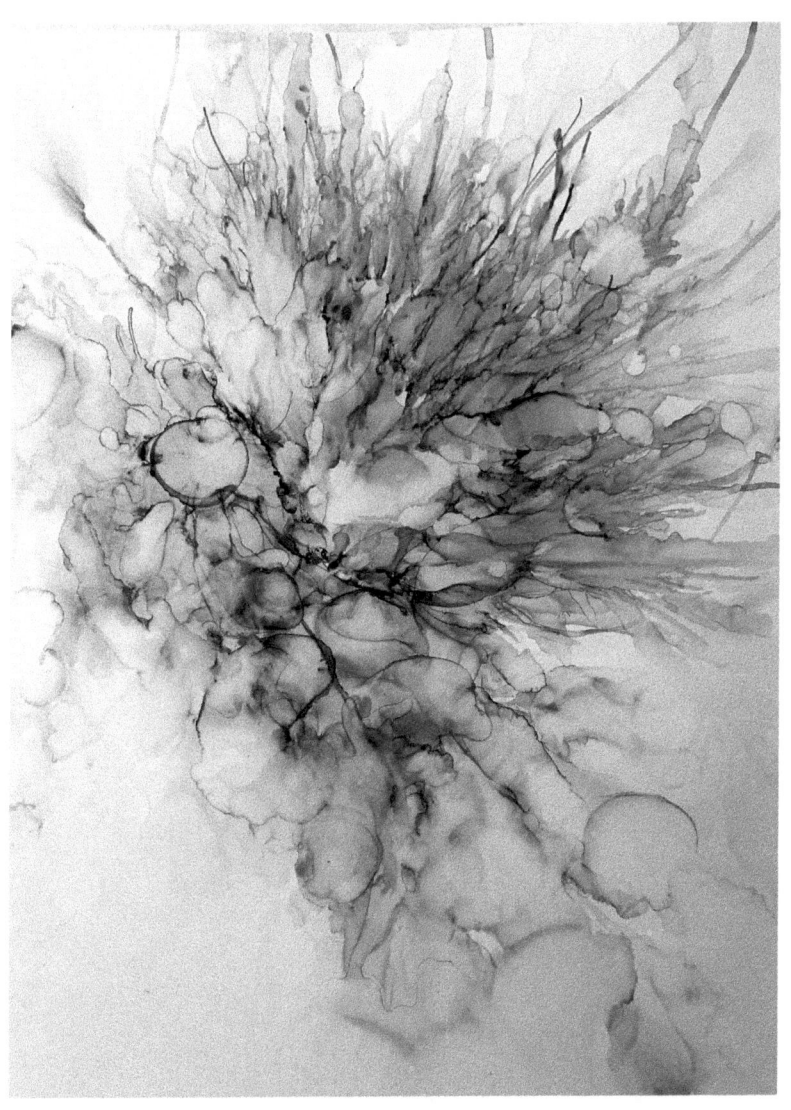

Contents

List of figures   xi
List of tables   xii
List of boxes   xiii
Series editor foreword by Simon Hayhoe   xiv
Preface   xvii

1 **A new way of seeing and conducting educational research**   1

    The arts and research 1
    Opportunity for relationship building and multiple modes of expression 3
    From representationalism to performativism 4
    Accounting for psychodynamics in educational research 6
    Connecting materiality to embodied experience 7

2 **Ontological, epistemological, and axiological foundations**   11

    Ontology, epistemology, and axiology 11
    Ontological stance: relational materialism 12
    Epistemological stance: critical realism 13
    Axiological stance: epistemic equality 15

3 **Research designs, preparation, and ethical considerations**   20

    Research designs for arts-based research in education 20
    Collage-making for educational research 21
    Research preparation 21
    Visual-narrative inquiry 24
    Ethical considerations 26

4 Research rigour and data collection 32

Research rigour 32
ENABLES project 35
Project on distributed leadership in Finnish and Chinese schools 36
Things to be considered 44

5 Reporting, interpreting, and discussing findings 46

Reporting findings 46
Interpreting and discussing findings 50

6 Impact of arts-based research methods and controversies surrounding them 54

Using arts-based methods to enrich close-to-practice research 54
Using arts-based methods to decolonise knowledge 55
Using arts-based research to inform or change education policies 56
Controversies surrounding arts-based research methods 57

7 Future development and conclusion 62

Further theorising arts-based research methods 62
Incorporating artistic techniques in empirical studies 63
Using arts-based methods as a form of activism 64
Conclusion 66

Index 71

Figures

1.1	A gold-plated PhD sword displayed on a wooden holder	2
3.1	Collage materials used in a research project in Finnish schools. A selection of collage materials and six pieces of blank A4-sized papers on the table for collage-making	23
3.2	Example of a research invitation. A one-page research invitation designed by the author. It contains information in layman's terms about the project name, the collage-making workshop purpose, and dos and don'ts during the collage-making. By the end of the poster, the researcher's contact information and date were listed	27
4.1	Collage made by LF1	37
4.2	Collage made by TF1	38
4.3	Collage made by LC1	40
4.4	Collage made by TC1	41
4.5	Resource–agency duality model of distributed leadership (Tian, 2016, p. 18)	43

Tables

4.1 Examples of collages and interview transcripts 37
5.1 Example of formative findings based on collages 47

Boxes

3.1	Examples of collage workshop preparation questions	21
3.2	Examples of follow-up interview questions after the collage-making	25
3.3	Example of an informed consent form	28

Series editor foreword
by Simon Hayhoe

Over 300 years ago, the enlightenment philosopher John Locke (2001) stated that we are born tabula rasa, that is to say an empty slate on which the story of our life begins its narrative. As a baby, our first forms of learning and analysis on this empty slate are sketched powerfully through our senses. Before we can speak, and certainly before we can write and form notional conscious ideas, we place objects in our mouth, we pay attention to the sounds around us, we touch objects in our immediate vicinity, and we are cuddled and smell those we can love and trust the most in our lives. Through these actions, we not only learn about our environment but also build the data on which our first exploration of the world is developed, a raw and primitive form of data that connects us to the world beyond our intellect.

Although our senses are imperfect and can be fooled easily, and we can never be sure that what we see is what others see (Popper, 1998), the visual representation of the world outside through icons of what we see is still our most reliable source of psychological data. This is because visual data defies the change to imagery that make these signs look nothing like that which they seek to represent. For it is only when we try to turn visual icons of our surroundings into an abstraction of what we see through semiotics, into crude symbols such as letters or numbers, that we start reducing the intrinsic information content of data. As Umberto Eco argues,

> Semiotics is in principle the discipline studying everything which can be used in order to lie. If something cannot be used to tell a lie, conversely it cannot be used to tell the truth: it cannot in fact be used "to tell" at all.
>
> (Eco, 1976, p. 7)

This is perhaps why visual data and the visual methodologies that are developed systematically is arguably the oldest form of data collection and analysis in our human history. It is moreover shown that it is the sense we rely most upon, with our brain trusting visual data over that of any other sensory data (Colavita, 1974). Thus, it seems reasonable to assume why our use of visual methodology to record and analyse human behaviour, thought and ideology not only predates philosophy and science, but it can also be said to predate written language. Visual data drawn on the walls of caves using a system of symbolic representation of activities tens of thousands of years ago gives us a glimpse into the world of our earliest human ancestors. The systematised graphics showed hunting parties possibly to map the area or techniques that were the techniques by which they hunted.

And yet, and yet.

Visual data and visual methodology are the first representations of civilisation and thus the first philosophy of human behaviour, culture, and society. Thus, it can be said that the earliest form of academic analysis was a form of social science that used visual methodology. In turn, these early drawings also allow us to speculate about other issues depicted through these early hunting practices, such as early religious rites, the movement of animals, and even the study of star systems in relation to human movement.

Despite this impeccable pedigree, the use of visual data was largely rejected by many forms of scientific study for millennia. As soon as images became transformed into writing, prose, poetry, and mathematics, and deductive logic was prized over inductive evidence, visual data was unreasonably looked down upon by *the educated*. Moreover, visual methodology was pompously disregarded by all but those who sought to develop technologies, medicine and the classification of nature that would change our world and our fortunes through designs and illustrations. Thanks to Plato and those that followed him who worshipped the unequalness of elitist philosophies over the evidence of our very eyes, it was even disbelief over observation that favoured the minority ruling classes over the majority. This was an unethical social movement that lasted almost 2,000 years in Western scientific philosophy and one that intellectuals and graphists such as Leonardo da Vinci (2008) scorned to no avail. Thus, only after a more widespread democratic movement has it only recently been accepted that images and graphics can be discussed and studied as a serious form of inductive data and visual knowledge, and a relatively modern endeavour being undertaken to promote visual methodology as a serious intellectual topic.

Subsequently, what follows in Dr Tian's book is vital for educational research. Although edited books have previously been published on visual methods in education, Meng Tian's book is particularly welcome and important as it is the first monograph on visual methods in the study of education. This is an important step forward in the maturation of 'the visual' as a form of systematic analysis in our subject, as it represents a single philosophy of visual methodology with representative examples. What follows in this carefully thought through volume also allows different dimensions and representations of visual data and representations of visual analysis and communication of different forms of data, including words and numbers.

Furthermore, Meng Tian's book also represents her international and intercultural experience of developing visual methodology. From her academic training in China and Finland, to her research career in Switzerland and the United Kingdom, Dr Tian has unrivalled experience in the development research methodology. And, now at the University of Birmingham, Dr Tian is a skilled and expert practitioner in the field of visual research, having used her methodology in many aspects of educational research. In this respect, I have no doubt that the following book will make a significant contribution to the debate on educational research methodology for decades to come and is a significant contribution to our book series on Visual and Qualitative Methods in Education.

References

Colavita, F. B. (1974). Human sensory dominance. *Perception & Psychophysics*, *16*, 409–412.

da Vinci, L. (2008). *Leonardo da Vinci notebooks* (T. Wells, Ed.). Oxford University Press.

Eco, U. (1976). *A theory of semiotics*. Indiana University Press.

Locke, J. (2001). *An essay concerning human understanding* (J. W. Yolton, Ed.). Everyman Library/J.M. Dent.

Popper, K. (1998). *Conjectures and refutations: The growth of scientific knowledge*. Routledge.

Preface

Many years ago, I was gifted Alain de Botton and John Armstrong's book *Art as Therapy*. The book starts with a question: What is art for? From a philosopher's viewpoint, de Botton believes great artworks have the power to console us in the face of our everyday struggles and confusion. As a historian, Armstrong perceives artworks as transcending time and space, connecting us to historical figures and events. Being an avid art lover and museum-goer, I am addicted to the thrill that every piece of powerful art evokes in me. During a recent trip to the Museo del Prado in Madrid, I paid Francisco Goya's black paintings one more visit. When standing in front *The Dog* and meeting his gaze, I ponder whether it was the loneliness and despair of Goya I saw, or those of the dog, the Spanish people in the early 19th century or my own? What could I see through the dog's eyes into that vast emptiness? At that moment, an invisible but intimate space between me and the painting was created. This space held a plethora of feelings, imagination, and a silent dialogue between Goya, the dog, and me. A piece of art is only completed when the artist, the art, and the viewer engage in this space of meaning-making. Our different threads of lived experiences were woven into a new reality and gave meaning to this moment, a moment when words failed.

In the social sciences, the million-dollar question is how to investigate human beings' lived experiences. We have learned thus far that human beings are far too complex to be reduced to measurables and simplified causations. *You get what you measure* is both an oft-cited rule and something of a curse, leaving nuances, contexts, and human dynamics unattended or even ignored. For centuries, researchers have also been constrained by cognitive tools like academic language, abstract concepts, and deductive reasoning. These put research participants in an even more inferior position when they lack familiarity with these scientific terms to articulate their lived experiences.

This raises the following question: If we live our lives with the full engagement of our bodies, feelings, environments, and materials, why are we limited to using language to report our lived experiences in research? This book is my attempt to answer this question. The new thinking and inquiry tools I introduce are arts-based research methods. Educational researchers, educators as well as undergraduate and postgraduate students will find this book a reader-friendly introduction to the vast world of qualitative and visual methodologies. Complex academic concepts are explained in lay terms, and concrete examples of designing and conducting an arts-based research project are provided.

In this book, I want to become a friend who shares a similar passion for the arts and educational research. Good artwork and good research are similar: originality and creativity are key. Hence, I hope every reader will learn the fundamental principles of arts-based research methods from this book and take their own stances when designing and conducting research projects. Please treat all the examples in the book as mirrors rather than blueprints.

This book would not have been possible without many important people in my life. I offer special thanks to two aspiring thinkers and dear friends, Professor Philip A. Woods and Dr Amanda Roberts, who inspired me to incorporate collage-making into my research project and generously provided me with invaluable advice along the way. I have learned a great deal about post-humanism and embodiment from my mentor, Professor Carol A. Taylor, during our walks along the canals. A big thank you to Professor Khalid Arar, who invited me to share my thoughts on arts-based methodology with his PhD students at the Texas State University. Many thought-provoking questions I received from the audience further deepened my knowledge of the topic which is now recorded in this book. You are all at the vanguard of a revolution in research methodology. Following in your footsteps, many scholars, including me, have been able to see educational phenomena through the lens of art.

Words cannot express my gratitude to the series editors, Dr Simon Hayhoe and Dr Rita Chawla-Duggan. I will always remember our thought-provoking discussions on arts, grounded theory, and phenomenography at Society Café in the gorgeous Bath Old Town. Thank you for your warm invitation and candid encouragement. This book series will empower more academics to venture into uncharted waters and contribute knowledge to qualitative and visual methodologies.

I would also like to extend my sincere thanks to Routledge editors, Molly Selby, and Rhea Gupta. You patiently answered all my questions and provided the most professional editorial support. Because of you, this publication process has been enjoyable and smooth.

My deepest gratitude goes to my grandparents, Shunlan Tang and Jinrong Wang, and my mother, Yongbin Wang, who introduced me to the arts and taught me to appreciate the beauty of this world since the day I was born. Lastly, special thanks to my furry friend, Leo the cat, who offers endless emotional support and patiently listened to every chapter of this book before anyone else.

Meng Tian
2022-08-15 Birmingham, UK

1 A new way of seeing and conducting educational research

The arts and research

In Finland, there is a lovely tradition of awarding a PhD graduate a doctoral hat and a doctoral sword along with a formal degree certificate. At the university conferment ceremony, called *promootio* in Finnish, PhD holders put on black tailcoats/dresses, wear doctoral hats, and carry their doctoral swords to parade proudly through the city. The night before the formal promootio, a sword-whetting ceremony is held. The new graduates pour champagne on a hand-turned grindstone to polish their swords. The whole ceremony symbolises the new PhD holders becoming the defenders of truth and knowledge in the realm of academia.

Looking back at my own journey as an emerging educational researcher, I was motivated to pursue my PhD studies in Finland so that I could be part of this academic tradition—and also have a cool story to tell whenever guests spot the sword displayed on my counsel table (see figure 1.1). It is the symbolic meaning embodied in that very artefact, the sword, that shapes part of my professional identity. It goes beyond words and a degree certificate. It is the power of art.

In human history, visual arts, including 2D drawings and paintings as well as 3D sculptures and reliefs, existed long before the invention of languages. Creating visual arts through the mind's eye or imagination is a defining characteristic of the human species (Morriss-Kay, 2010). Ancient languages—such as Egyptian hieroglyphs dating to the 28th century BCE and Chinese Jia-Gu-Wen (i.e. bone-and-shell scripts) dating to the 20th century BCE—adopted similar ideas of using standardised drawings to signify meanings, which later developed into modern languages. In other words, human beings first learned to use visual arts to express their ideas: only afterwards did they develop languages. The arts are essential tools for human beings to explore and connect with the world.

DOI: 10.4324/9781003196105-1

Figure 1.1 A gold-plated PhD sword displayed on a wooden holder.
Source: Photograph by the author.

Despite the importance of the arts in human history and cognitive development, arts-based research methods have not been widely applied in social science. One explanation is that, since the 18th century, the Enlightenment drove scientists to view reason as the source of authority and legitimacy. Since then, philosophers as well as social scientists have relied heavily on reason to speculate, debate, define, and theorise social phenomena. It was precisely their insistence on the pre-eminence of reason that gave birth to various research methodologies based heavily in rational linear thinking and empirically verifiable data (Israel, 2006). The rigour of research is measured by how logical the arguments are, whether the same conclusions can be reached by the same inductive or deductive analysis, and to what degree the findings can be generalised to other contexts. Under this research paradigm, language and rational thinking are the two primary tools.

The transition from modernity (characterised by the Enlightenment) to postmodernity (marked by feminism, post-structuralism, and post-humanism) opens the door for more creative and interactive forms of data, such as the arts, to be used in social science. Under this postmodern research paradigm, the deep-rooted faith in objective knowledge is questioned, critical thinking is encouraged, binary oppositions (e.g. good vs. evil, subject vs.

object, true vs. false) are de-constructed, and diverse forms of data are celebrated (Somerville, 2007). The arts, once again, become a mode of enquiry.

Opportunity for relationship building and multiple modes of expression

When the Enlightenment drove philosophical and methodological discourses in the western world towards reason and rationality, indigenous scholars in Canada and Australia continued to view research through the lens of ceremony (Wilson, 2008). Wilson writes that 'relationships do not merely shape reality, they *are* reality' and that 'research by and for Indigenous peoples is a ceremony that brings relationships together' (pp. 7–8). This highlights the co-creation of the research topic, processes, and findings between the researcher and the research participants. Just as 'the purpose of any ceremony is to build stronger relationships or to bridge the distance between aspects of our cosmos and ourselves', a well-designed research project should enable the researcher and the research participants to gain insights into this world (p. 11).

Interestingly, Somerville (2007, p. 238) cites an Australian Aboriginal scholar, Chrissiejoy Marshall, who says that there is no one word in any Aboriginal language for the term *art* because 'paintings do not exist as Art but as a medium through which [a person] can express and communicate information'. If we see meaning as created from an assemblage of human and non-human factors, language is not our only medium of communication and interaction. The arts provide us with exciting opportunities to employ singing, dancing, painting, photography, storytelling, theatre, and the combination of them in research.

Each form of art creates a new mode of expression. Arts-based methods in educational research embrace multiple modes of expression for relationship building. Meaning can be embodied in human research participants as well as in the materials they choose to perform their ideas, feelings, and experiences in the time and space where the research takes place. Meaning is also embodied in the relationship constructed and continuously re-constructed by the researcher and the research participants throughout the research process. To capture all these complex and nuanced meaning co-creation processes, we, as educational researchers, need to carefully position ourselves in the realms of ontology, epistemology, and axiology.

Arts-based research methods are not an extension or a supplement to existing qualitative research methods. In fact, to use arts-based research methods properly, researchers need to acquire new lenses through which to view human beings, our bodies, languages, feelings, and relationships with the material world. In the following sections, I will present key concepts in the theorisation of arts-based research methods.

From representationalism to performativism

When designing a quantitative survey or a qualitative interview, it is a common practice for the researcher to ask the respondents to recall a specific lived experience. The process of recalling and retelling a lived experience is the traditional representationalist approach to research. According to Eisner (2008), one feature that distinguishes arts-based research methods from other qualitative enquiries is that arts-based research employs aesthetic tools to illuminate phenomena that are either unintelligible or difficult to articulate through other representational forms. Doing research in, with, and through the arts provides viable alternatives to linguistic-based data collection tools such as interviews, documents, and open-ended surveys (O'Donoghue, 2009). The development of arts-based research methods since the mid-1990s has been mainly focused on how well the arts represent lived reality (e.g. Barone & Eisner, 2012; Eisner, 1995, 1997, 2008; Finley & Knowles, 1995; Piantanida et al., 2003). Commonly used concepts, including validity, reliability, transferability, and comparability, are used to measure the rigour of arts-based research (O'Donoghue, 2009).

In educational research, there is an increasing interest in arts-based methods. It is not just a methodological option for arts teachers to study and teach arts. Researchers from other disciplines such as educational psychology, early childhood education, educational leadership, educational sociology, and pedagogical studies also contribute to the development of arts-based methodologies and their applications in empirical research.

As an educational leadership researcher, I applied arts-based research methods in my 2012–2016 research project comparing the manifestations of distributed leadership and power relations in Chinese and Finnish schools. Through that research project, I discovered that the research participants not only re-lived their school leadership experiences but also developed their understandings of leadership distribution and power relations with the aid of art materials. In the interview phase of the research, a number of research participants repeatedly mentioned that they started to think about professional and interpersonal relationships in their school in a new light when making art. Something new to them began to emerge from the art-making process. For them, arts-based research methods are more like a stimulation for transforming the reality than a reflection of lived experience. As Barad (2007, p. 50), citing Hacking, states: '[R]eflection is insufficient; intervention is key'. The art-making process is, therefore, a meaning-making process, a tool for transformation, and even a starting point for activism. I will discuss the impact of arts-based research methods in Chapters 6 and 7.

To return to the point I made earlier, arts-based research methods employ multiple modes of expression to build relationships. They offer tools for researchers and research participants to interact with the material world in ways that eventually enhance our understanding of reality. In contrast to many other qualitative approaches—for example, phenomenology—arts-based research methods do not adopt a representationalist view of science. Here representationalism refers to a philosophical position that suggests our mind can only perceive the mental images of material objects instead of objects themselves. We only have perceptual representations of our lived experiences in the world not the world itself. How accurately the mental images correspond to the objects is key in representationalism. This is not to say that linguistic and/or artistic representations of the studied phenomena are not needed. Rather, I argue that researchers' and research participants' understandings of the phenomena continue to develop along with the research process. Questions—for example, can you recall your interaction with your students in the past three months, and how did that interaction affect your teaching?—force research participants to define their professional life in one episode, leaving the context largely unattended. By solely relying on anecdotal and episodic evidence, educational researchers may miss out on the journey of how their research participants became who they are.

It is precisely the process of *becoming* rather than *being* that arts-based research aims to capture. Here I propose that arts-based research methods should be based on performativism instead of representationalism. Notably, performativity is not the same thing as performance (Barad, 2007). For example, drawing random lines on a piece of paper is performed, but it may not be performative. There is a lack of socio-culturally constructed meaning behind the aimlessly created image to shape the social identity of the artist.

Before we connect arts-based research to performativism, let us quickly review how performativity is studied in linguistics and gender research. Key theorists of performativity, such as Austin (2005), argue that performative language has the power to change the world. For instance, by speaking wedding vows, one changes one's marital status from single to married. This performative speech has a specific social function and is commonly recognised by other people in the same socio-cultural context. Butler (1997) further claims that our gender is constructed and continuously shaped by performative social acts, such as being labelled as male or female at birth. Our reality and identities are socially constructed through performativity.

Barad (2007, p. 133) points out that performativity 'is not an invitation to turn everything (including material bodies) into words; on the contrary, performativity is precisely a contestation of the excessive power granted to language to determine what is real'. Besides speech, other forms of performative action, such as art-making, can also exercise discursive power. Butler (1999) conceptualises performativity, in the words of Harman and Zhang (2015, p. 69), as 'the iterative corporal enactment of social identity, regulated by institutional and cultural discourses'.

Take one example from my own research project, which used arts-based research methods in an educational leadership study. One of the participants, a teacher who works in a school with a steep hierarchy and an authoritarian culture, created a pyramid-like collage with the school principal on the top, the teachers in the middle, and the students at the bottom. No artefacts were used to symbolise non-teaching school staff or parents. In her narrative, the teacher described the collage-making process and why she positioned everyone in the way shown in the picture. By visualising her relationship with other key members (i.e. the principal and students) of the school and the power distances between them, it became clearer to her how she constructed her social and professional identities. In her narrative, she started to critique the existing power structure and ponder what she could do to change it. Therefore, I contend that arts-based research methods do not reproduce lived realities but challenge, de-construct, and re-construct them. Arts-based research is grounded in performativism and it exercises discursive power.

Accounting for psychodynamics in educational research

Educational research is essentially about human beings. Any educational activity—whether classroom teaching, school leadership, curriculum reform, or teachers' professional development—arouses a wide range of feelings from school leaders, teachers, and students. In the 21st century, educational reforms and changes were introduced into schools with unprecedented speed. Such changes inevitably increase affective intensity in educational organisations (Dale & James, 2015). They also raise challenges for educational researchers to probe these fast-paced changes and their impact on school members.

Research on people in educational activities taps into their feelings. Positive feelings, such as happiness, excitement, gratitude, and contentment, might be aroused. Similarly, negative feelings, such as anger, sadness, fear, and anxiety, might awaken, too. To effectively explore research participants' psychodynamics, arts-based research methods have an affective containment function. This function creates a secure environment for research participants to express their lived experiences and feelings with the help of art materials. Here, I use Dale and James's (2015, p. 93) definition: '[a]ffective containment is the strategies and processes that enable feelings to be fully experienced and used productively during unwelcome organisational change'. James (2009) differentiates feelings from emotions. According to him, feelings are affects that are experienced, while emotions are affects that are displayed.

To investigate research participants' feelings about a particular educational phenomenon via interviews or surveys is challenging for three reasons. First, research participants tend to refrain from displaying their emotions in front of a researcher, even if their feelings are intense, due to concerns over social etiquette. Second, strict research ethical guidelines caution researchers not to trigger unpleasant feelings in research participants that may harm their physical or emotional wellbeing. Third, it is difficult for research participants to effectively express their feelings through organised language in an interview or through a categorical list of choices presented in a survey.

Nevertheless, arts-based research methods offer research participants an opportunity to externalise their feelings through art materials. Feelings are dynamic. Dale and James (2015) emphasise that feelings can be projected onto other individuals who then introject and act on the basis of them. When overloaded with projected feelings, recipients cannot distinguish them from their own feelings (James & Vince, 2001). My research experience shows that, when research participants projected their feelings onto external artefacts, it became easier for them to talk about complex relationships or an emotionally charged incident. Art materials become a medium for feelings, creating a safe middle ground for the researcher and research participants to discuss sensitive issues without being overwhelmed by each other's projected feelings. This is not to say that arts-based research methods will remove all kinds of emotional distress. However, they can, to some extent, mitigate uncomfortable feelings related to the research topic. This is the affective containment function of arts-based research methods. Wilfred Bion's (1961) original conceptualisation of affective containment referred to individuals regulating unpleasant feelings by projecting them onto other individuals (Guzman et al., 2017). By contrast, I adopt a post-humanist view and claim affective containment also takes place when individuals project feelings onto non-human artefacts, thereby making those feelings more bearable. Empathy plays a critical role in affective containment. Some scholars argue that there is a risk of over-empathising with other research participants and thus collapse the boundaries between the self and others in research (Boler, 1999; Rice et al., 2021). In Chapter 6 of this book, I will return to this topic again.

Connecting materiality to embodied experience

Arts-based research methods connect the material world with research participants' embodied experience. Here, materiality refers to 'how the physical characteristics of objects and environments act upon people to influence action and meaning-making' (Griswold et al., 2013, p. 345). In other words, materiality refers to what objects do to people, and material analysis investigates how this process works. This suggests that, besides human beings, objects can also exercise agency on human beings. This challenges the long-standing humanist ontologies and proposes a post-humanistic view (Rousell & Fell, 2018).

In educational research, the manner in which research participants encounter, interact, and interpret art materials is circumscribed by the external world. The body is not merely the container of the self. The mind—body dichotomy has been challenged by many qualitative researchers who believe that the body is both a representation of the self and a tool for creation (Ellingson, 2017). Another view of embodiment is that individuals use their bodies as mediums to experience the world and as a mode of being-in-the-world (Lala & Kinsella, 2011). Embodiment is not an unfamiliar concept for educational researchers. Scholars tend to agree that knowledge production is a lived experience that requires both cognitive and physical engagement. Although learning by doing is a widely practised educational philosophy, scholars have only recently paid attention to embodiment in the development of qualitative research methods (Lala & Kinsella, 2011). Benner (2000) argues that neglecting the body and its impact on meaning-making in research leads to studies that are silent on human experiences. Ellingson (2006, p. 299) echoes this, arguing that, by ignoring the body as a means of perceiving and accessing the world, qualitative research 'obscures the complexities of knowledge production and yields deceptively tidy accounts of research'.

To sum up, arts-based research methods aim to bring performativity, psychodynamics, materiality, and embodiment together. They challenge the power of words as the dominant, if not the only, way of expressing ideas in research. Solely relying on the power of words perpetuates the fallacy that what cannot be articulated is not real. Arts-based research methods acknowledge that the material world also contributes to meaning-making through the intra-action of language, body, material, and environment.

In Barad's (2007) theorisation of intra-action, being (e.g. language, body, material, and environment) is never alone and never acts alone. Agencies and meanings emerge from the assemblage of human and non-human factors (Verlie, 2020). Therefore, in educational research, arts-based research methods not only examine the arts created by the research participants, but they also examine the artists (i.e. the research participants), their languages, art materials, environments, cultural contexts, and the entanglement of all these factors that give meaning to their lived experiences. This calls for a careful re-examination of the ontological, epistemological, and axiological stances taken by educational researchers. I will dive into these topics in Chapter 2.

References

Austin, J. L. (2005). *How to do things with words.* Harvard University Press.
Barad, K. (2007). *Meeting the universe halfway: Quantum physics and the entanglement of matter and meaning* (Illustrated ed.). Duke University Press.
Barone, T., & Eisner, E. W. (2012). *Arts based research.* Sage. https://us.sagepub.com/en-us/nam/arts-based-research/book234540
Benner, P. (2000). The roles of embodiment, emotion and lifeworld for rationality and agency in nursing practice. *Nursing Philosophy, 1*(1), 5–19. https://doi.org/10.1046/j.1466-769x.2000.00014.x
Bion, W. R. (1961). *Experiences in groups: And other papers* (1st ed.). Tavistock.
Boler, M. (1999). *Feeling Power: Emotions and Education* (1st ed.). Routledge.
Butler, J. (1997). *Excitable speech: A politics of the performative.* Routledge.
Butler, J. (1999). *Gender trouble: Feminism and the subversion of identity* (1st ed.). Routledge.
Dale, D., & James, C. (2015). The importance of affective containment during unwelcome educational change: The curious incident of the deer hut fire. *Educational Management Administration & Leadership, 43*(1), 92–106. https://doi.org/10.1177/1741143213494885
Eisner, E. W. (1995). What artistically crafted research can help us understand about schools. *Educational Theory, 45*(1), 1–6. https://doi.org/10.1111/j.1741-5446.1995.00001.x
Eisner, E. W. (1997). The promise and perils of alternative forms of data representation. *Educational Researcher, 26*(6), 4–10. https://doi.org/10.3102/0013189X026006004
Eisner, E. W. (2008). Persistent tensions in arts-based research. In M. Cahnmann-Taylor & R. Siegesmund (Eds.), *Arts-based research in education: Foundations for practice* (pp. 16–27). Routledge. https://doi.org/10.4324/9781315796147-11
Ellingson, L. L. (2006). Embodied knowledge: Writing researchers' bodies into qualitative health research. *Qualitative Health Research, 16*(2), 298–310. https://doi.org/10.1177/1049732305281944
Ellingson, L. L. (2017). *Embodiment in qualitative research.* Taylor & Francis.
Finley, S., & Knowles, J. G. (1995). Researcher as artist/artist as researcher. *Qualitative Inquiry, 1*(1), 110–142. https://doi.org/10.1177/107780049500100107
Griswold, W., Mangione, G., & McDonnell, T. E. (2013). Objects, words, and bodies in space: Bringing materiality into cultural analysis. *Qualitative Sociology, 36*, 343–364. https://doi.org/10.1007/s11133-013-9264-6
Guzman, A. B. de, Valdez, L. P., Pascasio, B. N. D. C., Pascual, F. J. C., & Pelayo, S. C. (2017). When everything is under control: Chronicling the affective containment experiences of Filipino elderly in institutionalized settings. *Educational Gerontology, 43*(5), 226–237. https://doi.org/10.1080/03601277.2017.1279953

Harman, R. M., & Zhang, X. (2015). Performance, performativity and second language identities: How can we know the actor from the act? *Linguistics and Education, 32*, 68–81. https://doi.org/10.1016/j.linged.2015.03.008

Israel, J. I. (2006). *Enlightenment contested: Philosophy, modernity, and the emancipation of man 1670–1752*. Oxford University Press.

James, C. (2009). The psychodynamics of educational change. In A. Hargreaves, A. Lieberman, M. Fullan, & D. Hopkins (Eds.), *Second international handbook of educational change* (pp. 47–64). Springer Netherlands. https://doi.org/10.1007/978-90-481-2660-6_3

James, C., & Vince, R. (2001). Developing the leadership capability of headteachers. *Educational Management & Administration, 29*(3), 307–317. ERIC.

Lala, A. P., & Kinsella, E. A. (2011). Embodiment in research practices: The body in qualitative research. In *Creative spaces for qualitative researching* (pp. 77–86). Brill Sense. https://brill.com/view/book/edcoll/9789460917615/BP000009.xml

Morriss-Kay, G. M. (2010). The evolution of human artistic creativity. *Journal of Anatomy, 216*(2), 158–176. https://doi.org/10.1111/j.1469-7580.2009.01160.x

O'Donoghue, D. (2009). Are we asking the wrong questions in arts-based research? *Studies in Art Education, 50*(4), 352–368. https://doi.org/10.1080/00393541.2009.11518781

Piantanida, M., McMahon, P. L., & Garman, N. B. (2003). Sculpting the contours of arts-based educational research within a discourse community. *Qualitative Inquiry, 9*(2), 182–191. https://doi.org/10.1177/1077800402250928

Rice, C., Cook, K., & Bailey, K. A. (2021). Difference-attuned witnessing: Risks and potentialities of arts-based research. *Feminism & Psychology, 31*(3), 345–365. https://doi.org/10.1177/0959353520955142

Rousell, D., & Fell, F. (2018). Becoming a work of art: Collaboration, materiality and posthumanism in visual arts education. *International Journal of Education Through Art, 14*(1), 91–110. https://doi.org/10.1386/eta.14.1.91_1

Somerville, M. (2007). Postmodern emergence. *International Journal of Qualitative Studies in Education, 20*(2), 225–243. https://doi.org/10.1080/09518390601159750

Verlie, B. (2020). From action to intra-action? Agency, identity and "goals" in a relational approach to climate change education. *Environmental Education Research, 26*(9–10), 1266–1280. https://doi.org/10.1080/13504622.2018.1497147

Wilson, S. (2008). *Research is ceremony: Indigenous research methods*. Fernwood Publishing. https://eduq.info/xmlui/handle/11515/35872

2 Ontological, epistemological, and axiological foundations

Ontology, epistemology, and axiology

Before using arts-based research methods, educational researchers should establish clear methodological forethought in their research designs. As outlined in Chapter 1, arts-based research methods are premised on a different understanding of human beings and our relationship with language, the body, art materials, and the environment. The underpinning ontological, epistemological, and axiological assumptions need to be clarified.

In a nutshell, ontology is a researcher's foundational theory of reality and the study of being. When establishing their ontological position, educational researchers answer question such as: What is considered reality? Does reality exist independently of the human beings who experience it? Do human beings construct reality? Can one person's reality be generalised universally or is it limited to a particular socio-cultural context (Leavy, 2014)?

In social science, different ontological stances fall on a continuum. On one end of the continuum, positivism claims that a real physical world exists independent of and external to the observer. Intangible values, beliefs, cultures, and experiences derive from the physical world but do not shape it. On the other end of the continuum, social constructivism contends that reality can only be understood via human beings and that the meaning of reality is always socially constructed (Denzin & Lincoln, 2017). All other ontological positions fall somewhere on the continuum between these two opposing views of reality.

Epistemology is concerned with the nature of knowledge and ways of knowing (Ponterotto, 2005). The relationship between the researcher (i.e. the knower) and knowledge is examined. There are three dominant and distinct epistemological principles. Empiricism states that knowledge comes only from sensory experience. All hypotheses have to be tested against observations and evidenced by observable results. If other researchers repeat the same research process, they ought to obtain the same results (Curd & Psillos, 2013). Interpretivism considers social reality as open to multiple interpretations and always shaped by an individual's historical, social, and cultural perspectives. There is no universal truth that can be acquired because research participants' subjectivity leads to different interpretations of reality (Cohen et al., 2017). Pragmatism admits there are multiple ways to acquire knowledge. Researchers can use subjective or objective techniques, or a combination of the two, in their research designs. As long as the methods yield knowledge and serve a practical purpose, they are deemed useful (Onwuegbuzie et al., 2009). Besides these three epistemological principles, researchers have proposed many other postmodern epistemologies, such as critical realism, post-humanism, and feminism.

Axiology refers to ethical and value issues involved in the research process. Researchers need to answer the following key questions: What are ethical and unethical behaviours in research? What is the relationship between the researcher and the research participants? Whose knowledge is valued? Who decides what is to be included in the research findings and why? How does the researcher secure research participants' privacy and protect their physical and emotional wellbeing?

In recent years, it has become paramount for educational researchers to answer these key questions in ethics forms before they approach potential research participants. For example, the *Ethical Guidelines for Educational Research* published by the British Educational Research Association (BERA, 2018) is a useful document for educational researchers to meet the highest ethical standards in all contexts.

In addition to satisfying the requirements of one's research ethics committee, researchers should always adhere to ethical principles to protect the rights, dignity, and wellbeing of research participants. Especially in educational research, many research participants, such as under-aged children and students with special needs, are considered vulnerable. Informed consent from their guardians and/or medical advisors must be acquired.

Close-to-practice research in education has gained much popularity in recent years. Many school leaders and teachers conduct research in their own schools to improve certain educational practices. This means many people are wearing two hats: that of the researcher and that of the school leader/teacher. The researcher–participant relationship, when combined with the leader–teacher or teacher–student relationship, may exacerbate already existing power imbalances. All these ethical concerns and solutions should be explicitly addressed in the ethics review.

Ontological stance: Relational materialism

In this book, I propose a relational materialist ontology for arts-based research. Relational materialism focuses on the relation between human and non-human materials, contending that subjectivity and agency emerge from the intra-action of their entanglement (Somerville, 2007; Verlie, 2020). According to Barad's (2007) conceptualisation of intra-action, the researcher, the research participants, the body, knowledge, language, the art materials, and the environment are not static and separable entities that exist independently in the world. Rather, these human and non-human factors are always already entangled with each other to produce meaning and agency in a dynamic way. Knowledge in relational materialist ontology cannot be bracketed out. This challenges Husserl's (1931) phenomenological ontology, which states that the essence of any phenomenon exists independently of human beings. It also challenges the anthropocentric view that the human being is always at the centre of qualitative research and is the only subject that can exercise agency (Roelvink & Zolkos, 2015).

Verlie (2020, p. 1270) reminds us that, in relational materialism, 'knowing, being, and doing are not so neatly separated'. When using arts-based research methods in educational research, researchers do not treat the arts, the school context, and the research participants with their narratives, their bodies, languages, and personal experiences as separate entities allowing researchers to verify different sources of information through triangulation. In contrast, researchers should focus on how these human and non-human factors invoke, challenge, and respond to each other, because it is their entanglement that gives meaning to studied educational phenomena.

Prior to arts-based research being conducted, many participants do not necessarily possess a well-thought-out, ready-made understanding of the research topic. In some cases, participants only start to think about certain topics when being asked specific questions. In that meaning-making process, research participants' senses, bodies, and memories work with and through the art materials. Hence, participants' understandings of the studied topic emerge into existence through complex and dynamic relationships of human and non-human entanglement (Barad, 2007). As Donati (2010, p. 98) concludes, 'social reality is social relationality'. Arts-based research methods are grounded in the view that social reality is an open, not a closed, system: that it is dynamic, not static, and relational, not isolated.

Epistemological stance: Critical realism

In my theorisation, arts-based research methods are built upon the convergence of relational materialism and critical realism. Through these two lenses, researchers can identify different layers of reality and ways to probe into them.

First, they both distinguish the real, the actual, and the empirical world. The real world is the broadest domain that exists independent of human perceptions or conceptions. It entails underlying laws, mechanisms (e.g. causal relationships), and structures that generate actual events. Within the real world, the actual world contains the various events and their effects that are caused by the mechanisms (Lawson et al., 1998). Admittedly, I hesitate to use the word 'mechanism' here, as it suggests a Newtonian mechanical view whereby everything is measurable and predictable in a determinist fashion. Nonetheless, I have retained the word out of respect for its usage in the original texts. Within the actual world, the empirical world consists of observable events and experiments that can be scientifically examined to help human beings understand the underlying mechanisms of natural and social reality (Bhaskar, 1978; Haigh et al., 2019). Echoing McNiff (2019), I agree that arts-based research methods allow research participants to use individualised artistic expressions of their perceived reality. Nevertheless, the research process is empirical. Art is not the ultimate point of the research but rather the vehicle of enquiry. As I stated in Chapter 1, art-making process is a meaning-making process, a tool for transformation, and even a starting point for activism.

Second, both relational materialism and critical realism acknowledge the emergence of agency and knowledge through entanglement or social relations (Archer, 2010). Human beings' understandings of a social phenomenon can change; thus, knowledge is transitive. In educational research, concepts and their meanings continue to develop as the result of practices, educational policies, social norms, societal values, and dynamic human actions. For example, researchers acknowledge the existence of 'learning' in the real world. However, they also acknowledge that, in different time periods and across different cultures, people's understandings of 'learning' have developed and continue to develop. Due to the emergent and transitive nature of knowledge, arts-based research methods do not aim to produce fixed and absolute knowledge but to capture the process of knowledge production.

Third, both relational materialism and critical realism perceive social reality as a complex and open system. To navigate increasingly complex challenges in education, researchers can no longer rely on the traditional reductionist methods that break a complex problem into bitesize pieces and solve them separately (Andersen et al., 2000). Philosophers of complexity theory criticise the deterministic and reductionist worldview for making people believe that control, measurement, and predictability are the only scientific ways to investigate the world (Boulton et al., 2015). Instead, complexity theorists embrace a kaleidoscope-like view of social reality, exploring how interdependent factors self-organise to create meaning and agency in a way that is shaped—but not determined—by history.

Embracing complexity in research means neither the researcher nor the research participants have total control over the research process; after all, they are parts of a complex, indeterministic system. Arts-based research methods bring more variables to the open system: art materials. Scholars have found that researchers' choices of art materials affect the forms of intra-action between humans and materials (Bagley & Castro-Salazar, 2012; Leavy, 2014). For instance, when incorporating watercolours in research, participants have less control over the materials because water, paper, and colour pigments often merge and flow independently of participants' original intentions (Krahnke & Gudmundson, 2019). In contrast, when participants use materials such as coloured feathers, beads, toothpicks, and straws to make collages, they have more control over the assemblages of these materials. Moreover, different participants may assign different meanings to the same object in their collages.

Axiological stance: Epistemic equality

Axiology refers to the nature of ethics and values in research. As argued earlier, arts-based research methods in educational research adopt a relational materialist ontology and a critical realist epistemology. Educational researchers who adopt these stances perceive the world as a complex open system in which human beings' understanding of the world is expressed through intra-active events consisting of both human and non-human factors. These positions demand that researchers define their relationship to research participants.

In qualitative research, it is often taken for granted that the researcher has a privileged knowledge position (Råheim et al., 2016). The inherent power imbalance between the researcher and the research participants is mitigated by the researcher's reflexivity. Here, reflexivity refers to a researcher being frank about and self-aware of any of their personal biases, beliefs, and judgements that may exert an impact on the research participants and the findings. In contrast to the traditional researcher-centric view, arts-based research methods allow knowledge and agency to emerge from the intra-action of the researcher, the research participants, the art materials, and the environment. This calls for a re-examination of researcher-centred epistemic authority in the qualitative research tradition. Here I want to highlight two aspects of axiology: procedural ethics and relational ethics.

Procedural ethics requires educational researchers to obtain approval from relevant ethics committees before conducting arts-based research with human participants. The potential physical and mental risks to research participants should be carefully evaluated by the researcher. For example, the researcher should assess whether certain art materials are toxic, dangerous, or provocative in ways that may cause research participants physical or emotional distress.

It is also essential to assess whether certain art materials contain symbolic meanings. For example, in certain cultures, a red star might be associated with Communism. These materials may not cause direct harm to research participants. However, they may influence the participants to associate the research topic with particular ideologies or beliefs, thereby having an impact on the research findings.

In response, the researcher should specify strategies to mitigate these potential risks and biases in the ethics form. Materials containing toxic substances such as hazardous air pollutants, formaldehyde, mercury, and lead should be excluded from the research. Ideally, suggestive materials such as religious symbols should also be eliminated because they may affect research participants' interpretations of the material and their agency in the art creation process. Especially in comparative studies, such biases may compromise the rigour of the entire research project. Of course, the researcher cannot foresee all the possible implicit meanings embedded in the selected art materials or how the participants might interpret them. Patterns of meaning interpretation only emerge from the data analysis at a later stage. In these cases, the researcher should capture these culture or group-specific meaning-making patterns, discuss their impact on the research findings, and provide suggestions as to whether to include or exclude certain art materials in future research.

When approaching research participants, the researcher should provide a consent form written in layman's terms. This consent form should detail the research purpose, questions, process, participants' rights, as well as data collection, storage, and usage. Research participants should be given sufficient time to read the consent form and ask questions. Signed consent forms should be stored—for instance, in a locked file cabinet—to protect participants' identities. Normally, signed consent forms are to be retained for a minimum of 2 to 3 years after the completion of the study (Clift & Camic, 2015).

In arts-based research, the intra-action of the researcher, the research participants, the environment, and the art materials is where feelings, meanings, and agency emerge. Thus, the researcher should carefully design the data collection methods to record this information-rich process. Ideally, video recording should be used because it records more information than audio recording. Some research participants may not want to be video recorded for reasons of confidentiality. I propose two solutions that may ease the participant's concerns. One is to avoid video recording the participant's face. The researcher can set the video camera in such a way that it only captures the participant's hand movements and the processes of selecting, making, and analysing the artworks. The researcher can take field notes to document the participant's facial expressions and expressed emotions.

Another solution is to have the research participant wear a helmet mounted by an action camera. This records the participant's perspective when they engage in the research process without exposing their face. When reviewing the recording, this method allows the researcher to step into the participant's shoes and, to some extent, capture nuances. For example: What is the first item that captures the participant's attention? How long does it take for the participant to create an artwork? Which part of the artwork is created first and which part last? How does the participant manoeuvre the art materials? The researcher can also review the video with the participant and probe into these nuances that only existed on the subconscious level before the discussion.

Relational ethics deals with the power relation between the researcher and the research participants. Bourriaud (2002) reminds us that art creation is a shared social and interactive encounter rather than an independent and private space. As mentioned earlier, our centuries-long research tradition tends to assign the researcher to the knowing position and the research participants to the not-knowing position. In arts-based research methods, however, these default knowledge positions are shifted.

The researcher is co-creating knowledge about the research topic together with the research participants by providing visual stimuli (e.g. art materials), thought-provoking open questions, and an emotionally safe space. In other words, the researcher does not confront the research participants as the knower with the aim of testing participants' knowledge of the topic. Instead, both the researcher and the participants are knowers but with different lived experiences. The art-making process is a shared meaning-making process where a group of knowers co-produce a variety of insights on a certain topic. Showing respect to the research participants and acknowledging them as knowledge contributors are key for trust building. By doing so, the researcher can, for example, tell the participants that the purpose the research project is not to judge whether their artworks are pleasing to the eye. Instead, it is the embodied meaning and the meaning-creation process that are at the core of the research.

The research process is structured but not tightly controlled. Although I advocate for equal epistemic status between the researcher and the research participants, it is essential that the researcher prepares a set of questions to guide the art-making and discussion. These questions should contain as little jargon as possible; any necessary jargon should be explained by the researcher in layman's terms (Leavy, 2017). In addition to discussing the artworks and their meanings, some meta questions on the art-making and meaning-making process should be incorporated into the discussion. These meta questions might be: What first came to your mind when you heard about topic x? Why did you choose this object to symbolise x? How does this art-making process make you feel? Does this object contain special meaning to you? Where do you locate yourself in this artwork? As knowledge co-creators, research participants should also be given time and space to raise questions and suggest new research perspectives.

Sometimes, arts-based research methods are employed in a group setting. This might be one researcher working with a group of research participants. In this context, one relational ethics challenge is how to deal with the power dynamics among the participants. Take a group of school teachers as an example. During the research process, perhaps one or two teachers are deemed superior to other participants in terms of their professional knowledge and/or leadership positions. They may dominate intra-action with other participants and turn the art-making space into an echo chamber. When this happens, discussions can quickly slide into the giving of generalised, standardised answers.

Because arts-based research methods tap into one's unique experiences and feelings, research participants may experience a certain level of vulnerability (Råheim et al., 2016). They may hesitate to express this vulnerability because it may cast a shadow on their professional identity in front of the researcher and their peers. To address this challenge, the researcher should practice reflexive awareness. Before commencing the research, it is necessary to conduct an analysis of the sensitivity of the research topic and any possible subtopics. For early career educational researchers, receiving advice from senior researchers or other research team members can be beneficial. If there are time and resource constraints, the researcher can conduct arts-based research in smaller groups (e.g. four to five participants) and protect every participant's right to make a knowledge contribution to the project.

References

Andersen, P. B., Christiansen, P. V., & Emmeche, C. (Eds.). (2000). *Downward causation: Minds, bodies & matter*. Aarhus University Press.

Archer, M. (2010). Critical realism and relational sociology. *Journal of Critical Realism*, 9(2), 199–207. https://doi.org/10.1558/jcr.v9i2.199

Bagley, C., & Castro-Salazar, R. (2012). Critical arts-based research in education: Performing undocumented historias. *British Educational Research Journal*, 38(2), 239–260. https://doi.org/10.1080/01411926.2010.538667

Barad, K. (2007). *Meeting the Universe Halfway: Quantum Physics and the Entanglement of Matter and Meaning* (Illustrated ed.). Duke University Press.

Bhaskar, R. (1978). *A realist theory of science*. Harvester.

Boulton, J. G., Allen, P. M., & Bowman, C. (2015). *Embracing complexity: Strategic perspectives for an age of turbulence*. Oxford University Press.

Bourriaud, N. (2002). *Relational aesthetics*. Les Presses du réel.

British Educational Research Association. (2018). *Ethical guidelines for educational research*. British Educational Research Association. www.bera.ac.uk/publication/ethical-guidelines-for-educational-research-2018

Clift, S., & Camic, P. M. (2015). *Oxford textbook of creative arts, health, and wellbeing: International perspectives on practice, policy and research*. Oxford University Press.

Cohen, L., Manion, L., & Morrison, K. (2017). *Research methods in education* (8th ed.). Routledge.

Curd, M., & Psillos, S. (Eds.). (2013). *The Routledge companion to philosophy of science* (2nd ed.). Routledge.

Denzin, N. K., & Lincoln, Y. S. (2017). *The SAGE handbook of qualitative research.* SAGE Publications.

Donati, P. (2010). *Relational sociology: A new paradigm for the social sciences* (1st ed.). Routledge.

Haigh, F., Kemp, L., Bazeley, P., & Haigh, N. (2019). Developing a critical realist informed framework to explain how the human rights and social determinants of health relationship works. *BMC Public Health, 19*(1), 1571–1583. https://doi.org/10.1186/s12889-019-7760-7

Husserl, E. (1931). *Ideas: General introduction to pure phenomenology.* Macmillan.

Krahnke, K., & Gudmundson, D. (2019). Learning from Aesthetics: Unleashing untapped potential in business. In P. Leavy (Ed.), *Handbook of arts-based research* (pp. 559–571). Guilford Press.

Lawson, T., Collier, A., Bhaskar, R., Archer, M., & Norrie, A. (1998). *Critical realism: Essential readings* (1st ed.). Routledge.

Leavy, P. (2014). *The Oxford handbook of qualitative research.* Oxford University Press.

Leavy, P. (2017). *Handbook of arts-based research.* Guilford Publications.

McNiff, S. (2019). Philosophical and practical foundations of artistic inquiry: Creating paradigms, methods, and presentations based in art. In P. Leavy (Ed.), *Handbook of arts-based research* (pp. 22–36). Guilford Press.

Onwuegbuzie, A. J., Johnson, R. B., & Collins, K. M. (2009). Call for mixed analysis: A philosophical framework for combining qualitative and quantitative approaches. *International Journal of Multiple Research Approaches, 3*(2), 114–139. https://doi.org/10.5172/mra.3.2.114

Ponterotto, J. G. (2005). Qualitative research in counseling psychology: A primer on research paradigms and philosophy of science. *Journal of Counseling Psychology, 52*(2), 126–136. https://doi.org/10.1037/0022-0167.52.2.126

Råheim, M., Magnussen, L. H., Sekse, R. J. T., Lunde, Å., Jacobsen, T., & Blystad, A. (2016). Researcher—researched relationship in qualitative research: Shifts in positions and researcher vulnerability. *International Journal of Qualitative Studies on Health and Well-Being, 11.* https://doi.org/10.3402/qhw.v11.30996

Roelvink, G., & Zolkos, M. (2015). Affective ontologies: Post-humanist perspectives on the self, feeling and intersubjectivity. *Emotion, Space and Society, 14,* 47–49. https://doi.org/10.1016/j.emospa.2014.07.003

Somerville, M. (2007). Postmodern emergence. *International Journal of Qualitative Studies in Education, 20*(2), 225–243. https://doi.org/10.1080/09518390601159750

Verlie, B. (2020). From action to intra-action? Agency, identity and 'goals' in a relational approach to climate change education. *Environmental Education Research, 26*(9–10), 1266–1280. https://doi.org/10.1080/13504622.2018.1497147

3 Research designs, preparation, and ethical considerations

Research designs for arts-based research in education

Arts-based methods in educational research have multiple applications. Leavy (2017) synthesises the following genres: literacy (e.g. narrative inquiry, autoethnography, short story, fiction, poetry), performative arts (e.g. artography, dancing, ethnodrama, ethnotheatre), visual arts (e.g. drawing, painting, collage, installation art, comics), audio–visual arts (e.g. film, ethnocinema), and mixed-methods.

By integrating the human being's visual, emotional, intellectual, and psychological responses to the external world, arts-based research methods offer unlimited opportunities for educational researchers to create innovative research designs. Taylor and Gannon (2018) argue that posthumanist research methodologies, including arts-based research methods, reject the research object—research subject dichotomy. Instead, focus falls on the assemblages and relations of subjects and objects. Experimental work has explored this uncharted methodological terrain. Nevertheless, Taylor and Gannon (2018) further point out the discrepancy between the innovative data collection methods (e.g. collage making, storytelling, and ethnocinema) and the conventional data analysis approach (e.g. deductive analysis). More specifically, although some scholars may have experimented with novel data collection tools, in their writings they return to conventional deductive analysis and follow the reductionist tradition. This disparity calls for more nuanced research designs.

Arts-based research methods bridge the polarised arts and science (Leavy, 2017). In this book, I focus on the process of using collage-making for educational research. Due to limited space, other genres of art—such as literary art, performative art, audio—visual art, and mixed-methods of various forms of art—are not addressed. Nevertheless, I believe certain fundamental principles can be applied in a wider context.

DOI: 10.4324/9781003196105-3

Collage-making for educational research

The etymology of the word 'collage' derives from the French word *collé*, which means 'to glue' or 'to stick together' (Gerstenblatt, 2013, p. 294). In educational research, collage-making refers to the process of choosing and assembling fragments of images and art materials to form an image on blank paper that portrays the studied educational phenomena.

Collage-making has a special value for investigating the way we experience the world because of its aesthetic power to evoke feelings and the visualisation of intersubjective relations (Chilton & Scotti, 2014). Butler-Kisber and Poldma (2010) claim that collage-making has gained increasing popularity as a form of qualitative inquiry because it allows researchers to work in a non-linear and intuitive way. Butler-Kisber (2008, 2010) identifies three usages of collage-making in research: collage-making as a reflective process, as a form of elicitation, and as a way of conceptualising ideas. Echoing Chapter 1, collage-making can be used to tease out multiple perceptions, experiences, and interpretations of studied educational phenomena through the intra-actions of language, the body, material, and environment (Barad, 2007; Butler-Kisber, 2010). In the following section, I will explain the process of research preparation.

Research preparation

In contrast to drawing or painting, collage-making allows research participants to use minimum artistic transformations—such as cutting, tearing, assembling, and gluing—to express experiences and ideas through materials from everyday life (Roberts & Woods, 2018). Brockelman (2001) reminds us that, because collage materials are drawn from everyday life, they already contain certain meanings. When a research participant makes a collage, meaning is not created by an unrestrained act of the imagination, as it is with drawing or painting. Instead, meaning is created by constructing relationships among objects. Hence, a researcher should be aware of the implicit and explicit meanings contained in the collage materials at the research preparation stage.

To prepare for the collage-making process, the following questions can help the researcher:

Box 3.1 Examples of collage workshop preparation questions

1 Do I provide collage materials, or do I allow the research participants to bring their own materials?

2 Do I want to include materials that contain explicit meanings, such as a cut-out piece of text, a photograph, or a religious symbol (e.g. a cross, a six-pointed star)?
3 Do I want to include materials that contain implicit meanings? For example, a red star might be associated with the Communist Party in some countries, a crown might suggest formal authority, or the images of a stick and a carrot might denote punishment and reward. In some cultures, a picture of a burning candle might imply a self-sacrificing teacher or mother figure who burns herself to illuminate the path for the future generation.
4 To what degree do I allow the participants to transform the materials? For example, can they cut, tear, twist, draw/write on, assemble, and glue the materials?
5 Do I arrange the collage-making in a group setting or in a one-to-one setting? If in a group setting, do I provide equal access to sufficient materials for all participants, or do they select materials based on the 'first come, first served' principle?
6 Do I recycle the collage materials? If so, how do I make a record of the collage-making process and the final artworks?
7 Do I want the research participants to create one collage or a collection of collages that depict different facets and nuanced meanings of a studied phenomenon? (Butler-Kisber, 2010)
8 How much time do I give the research participants to make the collage?
9 How do I use visual-narrative inquiry to further probe into the studied phenomenon by, for instance, conducting follow-up interviews?
10 How do I inform the research participants about the research project, their rights, and the storage and usage of data?

Using my own research project on distributed leadership in Chinese and Finnish schools as an example, I will now depict my research preparation process by answering the above questions.

Figure 3.1 shows a picture of collage materials I prepared for a group of six research participants who attended one collage-making workshop in the 2014 research project. A research invitation and an informed consent form were distributed to each participant to explain the research purpose, the questions, the participants' rights of withdrawal and anonymity, the research process, and the storage and usage of data. Each participant was invited to make a collage that visualised their understandings and experiences of

Figure 3.1 Collage materials used in a research project in Finnish schools. A selection of collage materials and six pieces of blank A4-sized papers on the table for collage-making.

Source: Photograph by the author.

leadership distribution in the school. At the beginning of the workshop, I emphasised the following principles: First, there were no right or wrong answers to the questions. Second, the collages would not be judged in terms of aesthetic merit. The goal was not to make a piece of aesthetically pleasing artwork but a collage that embodied the participant's lived experiences and feelings. Third, participant's personal information and the school's name would remain confidential in the project and in any publications. Fourth, the collages and interview data would be used for research purposes only.

When purchasing the collage materials from local stationery shops, I avoided materials with texts or images that had suggestive meanings because their contents may have been taken literally, thereby restraining participants' freedom of thought and expression. Each workshop contained four to six participants with similar roles, such as senior leaders, teachers, non-teaching staff, and students. This allowed the within group and between group comparison. I provided all participants with equal access to ample collage materials.

The collage materials included multicolour papers, feathers, balloons, ribbons, plastic straws, plastic food picks, small net bags, handmade felt flowers, small-sized paper photo frames, sewing needle pins, and paper clips. Three scissors were provided for the participants to cut the materials. Each participant was given a piece of blank A4-sized paper to construct their collage on. Glue was not provided because I planned to recycle the materials after each workshop. Since the materials were not fixed on the paper, the participants were able to move them around when narrating their experiences (Roberts & Woods, 2018). The participants could use marker pens to draw images but not to write down words on the collage. This was because, at this stage, I wanted the participants to visualise their lived experiences of leadership in their school without engaging in language-based reasoning. Last but not least, a box of chocolates was shared to make the collage-making process more enjoyable.

The participants were allowed to chat with each other and with the researcher during the collage-making process. On average, the research participants finished their artwork within 20 minutes. When they had finished, I photographed each collage and conducted an interview with each participant, listening to their narratives of their artwork as well as the experience of collage-making. The collage-making and interview constituted the visual-narrative inquiry of this research project. In the following section, I will introduce the rationale of visual-narrative inquiry and the interview part of the data collection.

Visual-narrative inquiry

As discussed in Chapter 1, in this book I adopt the post-humanist paradigm to theorise arts-based research methods. I see meaning and agency as being created from the entanglement of the researcher, the research participants, language, non-human artefacts, and the environment (Barad, 2007; Rousell & Fell, 2018). Visual-narrative inquiry, according to this post-humanist paradigm, opens up avenues to comprehend this entanglement. The collage-making process constitutes the visual narration, while the subsequent interview gives research participants the opportunity to further explain the meanings, feelings, and lived experiences of the studied phenomena with the aid of visual stimuli (Roberts & Woods, 2018).

Echoing Roberts and Woods (2018), I agree that conducting an interview after collage-making is a better approach than conducting both simultaneously. One reason is that narrating one's lived experiences and feelings requires linear and logical thinking, which can be at odds with the non-linear intuitive thinking used in the collage-making process. Another reason is that the participants may feel more pressured when juggling two tasks at the same time (Roberts & Woods, 2018). The third reason is that, compared to materiality, 'language has been granted too much power' (Barad, 2007, p. 132). The sequential visual-narrative inquiry allows collage materials to exercise agency and to participate in the meaning-making process together with the research participants and the researcher. Lastly, because most research participants do not have the same level of familiarity with the terminologies and theories as the researcher does, they often feel inferior in front of the researcher. Conducting an interview after collage-making can break this researcher–participant power imbalance by shifting the focus to the artwork-stimulated narration. It is worth reiterating here that artworks (e.g. collages) are not merely representations of reality. The art-making process is a meaning-making process. Art materials, therefore, enable research participants to make sense of lived experiences and feelings, especially the ones that are unintelligible or unconscious to them. This process can also transform the research participants' understanding of the phenomena and start to re-imagine other possibilities.

Let us continue with the example of the distributed leadership research project in Chinese and Finnish schools. Except for the school senior leaders, the topic of leadership appeared alien to most teachers, non-teaching staff, and students. Many of them were not consciously thinking of how leadership was distributed, to whom, and why in their school before participating in this project. By making collages, some research participants reported that they started to think about how they were related to other school members and what roles they had played in leadership work. The collage materials gave them something tangible with which to visualise these interpersonal and interprofessional connections.

After the participants had completed collage-making, I asked the following questions in the one-to-one interview. You may tailor your interview questions to serve your particular research purposes. The guiding principle here is to respect research participants as knowledge contributors with an equal epistemic status to the researcher. I asked the participants the following questions listed in Box 3.2.

Box 3.2 Examples of follow-up interview questions after the collage-making

1. From the perspective of leadership structure and distribution, can you please describe the collage you just made?
2. Where do you see yourself in this collage? How are you related to other school members such as the principal, subject leaders, students, and non-teaching staff?
3. Why did you choose x (i.e. a particular artefact) to signify y (e.g. a particular role, person, work process, relationship, or scenario)? What meaning does this artefact convey?

> 4 Can you give me one example of how leadership was distributed to you or by you in the school? How did you feel during that leadership process?
> 5 How do you feel about this collage-making workshop?
> 6 Has your understanding of school leadership changed after the collage-making? If so, what have changed?
> 7 If you could change the current leadership distribution, what kinds of changes would you make and why?
> 8 Are there any particular details in the collage you want to elaborate on?

Compared to the traditional one-to-one interview format, this visual-narrative inquiry appears to be more effective and thought-provoking to the participants. The research participants are given more time to build rapport with the researcher and can use both visual and verbal channels to make sense of their lived experiences (Gerstenblatt, 2013). Next, I will bring a highly important topic to your attention: ethical considerations in arts-based research.

Ethical considerations

Despite the increasing popularity of arts-based research, few studies have examined ethical challenges and solutions in arts-based research in education. Health researchers who apply arts-based research methods have also found the ethical guidelines not explicit enough to support researchers (Clift & Camic, 2015; Water et al., 2020). Although general ethical regulations are applicable—such as the most recent 4th edition of the British Educational Research Association's (BERA's) *Ethical Guidelines for Educational Research*—more nuanced ethical considerations in arts-based research are needed.

When discussing research ethics, there are two major issues to be taken into consideration: procedural ethics and situational ethics (Guillemin & Gillam, 2004). Procedural ethics involves research committees reviewing and approving ethics forms as well as the researcher collecting research participants' informed consent. In recent years, research institutions and higher education institutions have developed research ethics governance principles and templates to guide this process. It is imperative for researchers to assess and to mitigate the potential physical, psychological, financial, and professional harms and risks faced by research participants. Only after the ethics form has been approved can a researcher start recruiting research participants.

When recruiting research participants, the researcher should distribute a research invitation accompanied by an informed consent form. The research

Research designs, preparation, and ethical 27

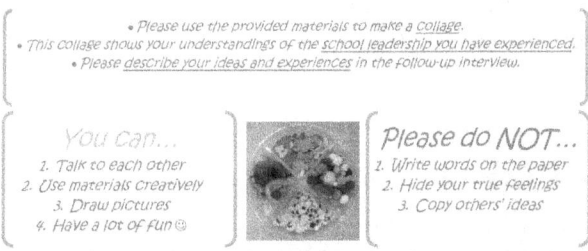
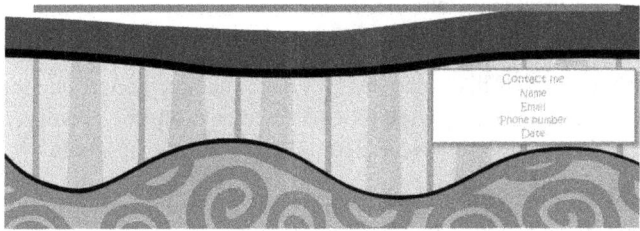

Figure 3.2 Example of a research invitation. A one-page research invitation designed by the author. It contains information in layman's terms about the project name, the collage-making workshop purpose, and dos and don'ts during the collage-making. By the end of the poster, the researcher's contact information and date were listed.

invitation comprises a concise summary of the project purpose, data collection procedure, and sometimes a 'Dos and Don'ts Guide' for participants (see Figure 3.2). Normally, the research invitation does not exceed one page in length and might contain eye-catching pictures and fonts to attract participants' attention. The consent form introduces the research aims, procedure, participants' rights, and data protection and usage rules (see Box. 3.3). Both the research invitation and the informed consent form should be written in layman's terms. In addition, it is advisable to explain the research project orally and to encourage research participants to ask clarification questions.

Figure 3.2 and Box 3.3 are examples of the research invitation and the informed consent form from the project I conducted. Please note that both the English and Finnish versions of these documents were provided to ensure participants' full understanding of the project. Because this project is a comparative study. There is also a Chinese version used to collect data in Chinese schools. In addition to these, I completed a separate ethics form and received approval from the Faculty of Education at the university I was affiliated with. All the ethics forms and signed consent forms were kept for 24 months after the data collection.

Box 3.3 Example of an informed consent form

Distributed Leadership in Chinese and Finnish Schools Informed Consent Form

Research aims: This project aims to visualise school leaders', teacher's, non-teaching staffs', and students' experiences and feelings about leadership structure and distribution in the school.

Methodology: This study uses collage-making and a one-to-one interview as data collection tools. The collage will be photographed and the interview audio-recorded for data analysis purpose.

Research procedure: The research project entails:

- Participation in a collage-making workshop about my experiences and feelings of leadership in the school I work for/study in. (About 15 to 20 minutes.)
- Participation in a one-to-one interview to describe the meaning of the collage and my experience of the collage-making workshop. (About 25 to 30 minutes.)

By signing and returning this form I confirm the following:

1. I have read this information sheet and understand the purpose of the study and my role as a participant.
2. I understand that my participation is voluntary and that I can withdraw by informing the researcher during the workshop and interview without giving a reason and without penalty.

3 I understand that after 10 days from the workshop day my personal data (including name, email address, and school) will be anonymised to ensure research confidentiality. After that, my data cannot be withdrawn from the project.
4 I understand that my collage and interview data will be used for research and teaching purposes, including lectures, seminars, workshops, reports, publications, and conference presentations.
5 I understand that I and the researcher own the copyright of the artwork I create during the workshop. The researcher can publish my artwork for teaching and research purposes.
6 I understand that I can choose not to share or speak about sensitive experiences that may cause professional or psychological harm to me.
7 I understand that my collage will be photographed and my interview audio-recorded by digital devices (i.e. a smart phone and a digital camera).
8 I understand that I will be visible to other participants in the workshop but that the researcher and all the participants agree not to share participants' personal information beyond the workshop.
9 I understand that the artwork I create will not be assessed in terms of artistic merit.
10 I understand that all data will be stored on secure devices and servers for 24 months.
11 I have been given the opportunity to ask questions.

- I agree to participate in the study as outlined earlier.

If you have any questions, please contact XXX. If you wish to participate in the project, please provide your name, signature, and the date below and return the consent form to XXX.

Name of participant:

Signature:

Date:

In addition to procedural ethics, researchers should account for situational ethics. Situational ethics involves making ethical judgements and choices during the research process. In this section, I will discuss two examples of situational ethics. One involves children and young people in arts-based research, and the other regards the ownership and usage of copyright.

Like in health research, educational research often involves children and young people. On the one hand, researchers are obliged to seek approval from guardians or professionals who act as proxies for under-aged participants. On the other hand, researchers aim to accurately record children's and young people's voices free of censorship or interference from gatekeepers (Water et al., 2020). Arts-based research can minimise the restrictions caused by children's or young people's lack of vocabulary or verbal communication skills. Art stimuli can arouse their interest and make the art creation process fun (Carter & Ford, 2013). Therefore, arts-based research mitigates interference from guardians acting as children's or young people's spokespersons.

Child-centred and child-friendly arts-based research also involves using slow-paced language and illustrative examples to explain the research procedure, taking children's attention spans into consideration, and creating a physically and emotionally safe environment (Ford et al., 2007). Carter and Ford (2013) further suggest avoiding making arts-based research activities too complicated and allowing children and young people to select from a range of activities instead of limiting them to only one. Bringing non-research resources—such as toys, games, balloons, and puppets—can help build trust between the researcher and the participants. Thanking children and young people with a designed certificate can boost their enthusiasm. All these arrangements are ethically important moments in arts-based research.

The other situational ethics issue I discuss here is copyright. Some arts-based research projects allow participants to create original artworks, while others yield derivative works. A derivative work is the creative rearrangement of the elements of an underlying copyrightable work: For example, one that uses images or fragments from newspaper and magazines. To be protected by copyright, the derivative work should involve a substantial transformation, adaptation, or modification of the underlying work and demonstrate the research participant's independent and original ideas. Another approach is to use visual images and music from Creative Commons sources. According to Norris (2008), because most arts-based research projects are used for research and educational purposes, no legal cases surrounding copyright have occurred so far.

In the project I conducted, I purposefully avoided copyright issues by using everyday art materials from stationery shops. When designing arts-based research projects, researchers are advised to check the copyright laws in their countries. It is necessary to mention ownership and usage of the created artworks in the information sheet so that researchers can publish artworks as part of the research data (see Box 3.3).

References

Barad, K. (2007). *Meeting the universe halfway: Quantum physics and the entanglement of matter and meaning* (Illustrated ed.). Duke University Press.
Brockelman, T. P. (2001). *The frame and the mirror: On collage and the postmodern*. Northwestern University Press.
Butler-Kisber, L. (2008). Collage as Inquiry. In J. G. Knowles & A. L. Cole (Eds.), *Handbook of the Arts in Qualitative Research: Perspectives, Methodologies, Examples, and Issues* (pp. 265–277). SAGE Publications, Inc. https://doi.org/10.4135/9781452226545
Butler-Kisber, L. (2010). *Qualitative Inquiry: Thematic, Narrative And Arts-Informed Perspectives* (1st ed.). SAGE Publications Ltd.
Butler-Kisber, L., & Poldma, T. (2010). The power of visual approaches in qualitative inquiry: The use of collage making and concept mapping in experiential research. *Journal of Research Practice, 6*(2), Article M18.
Carter, B., & Ford, K. (2013). Researching children's health experiences: The place for participatory, child-centered, arts-based approaches. *Research in Nursing & Health, 36*(1), 95–107. https://doi.org/10.1002/nur.21517
Chilton, G., & Scotti, V. (2014). Snipping, gluing, writing: The properties of collage as an arts-based research practice in art therapy. *Art Therapy, 31*(4), 163–171. https://doi.org/10.1080/07421656.2015.963484
Clift, S., & Camic, P. M. (2015). *Oxford textbook of creative arts, health, and wellbeing: International perspectives on practice, policy and research*. Oxford University Press.
Ford, K., Sankey, J., & Crisp, J. (2007). Development of children's assent documents using a child-centred approach. *Journal of Child Health Care, 11*(1), 19–28. https://doi.org/10.1177/1367493507073058
Gerstenblatt, P. (2013). Collage portraits as a method of analysis in qualitative research. *International Journal of Qualitative Methods, 12*(1), 294–309. https://doi.org/10.1177/160940691301200114
Guillemin, M., & Gillam, L. (2004). Ethics, reflexivity, and "ethically important moments" in research. *Qualitative Inquiry, 10*(2), 261–280. https://doi.org/10.1177/1077800403262360
Leavy, P. (2017). *Handbook of arts-based research*. Guilford Publications.
Norris, J. (2008). Collage. In *The SAGE encyclopedia of qualitative research methods* (Vol. 1, pp. 94–97). SAGE Publications Ltd. https://uk.sagepub.com/en-gb/eur/the-sage-encyclopedia-of-qualitative-research-methods/book229805
Roberts, A., & Woods, P. A. (2018). Theorising the value of collage in exploring educational leadership. *British Educational Research Journal, 44*(4), 626–642. ERIC.
Rousell, D., & Fell, F. (2018). Becoming a work of art: Collaboration, materiality and posthumanism in visual arts education. *International Journal of Education Through Art, 14*(1), 91–110. https://doi.org/10.1386/eta.14.1.91_1
Taylor, C. A., & Gannon, S. (2018). Doing time and motion diffractively: Academic life everywhere and all the time. *International Journal of Qualitative Studies in Education, 31*(6), 465–486. https://doi.org/10.1080/09518398.2017.1422286
Water, T., Payam, S., Tokolahi, E., Reay, S., & Wrapson, J. (2020). Ethical and practical challenges of conducting art-based research with children/young people in the public space of a children's outpatient department. *Journal of Child Health Care, 24*(1), 33–45. https://doi.org/10.1177/1367493518807318

4 Research rigour and data collection

Research rigour

What constitutes high-quality arts-based research for education is a key issue under discussion in this book. Like many other qualitative research methods, the rigour of arts-based research is not determined by if an artwork can be reproduced if a certain research process is followed. In other words, repeatability and the traditional definition of reliability (i.e. the same research method produces stable and consistent results) are not applicable here as criteria for research rigour. In Chapter 1, I contend that arts-based research does not subscribe to representationalism but adopts a performative approach to recreate and reimagine different dimensions of phenomena. The research process is also a meaning-making process. Different forms of data, such as artwork, interviews and observations, are used not only to verify truthfulness but also to enrich research participant's understandings, feelings, and lived experiences.

The traditionalist view of using knowledge to enhance predictability and reduce uncertainty has been dominating educational research for decades. It is part of human nature to 'long for closure to the important issues, for resolution to events, for answers to nettlesome questions that plague our lives' (Barone, 2001, p. 24). In the traditional sense, research should be useful. Nevertheless, Barone (2001) rejected Mayer's (2000) predisposition of seeing arts-based research in education as non-scientific, arguing that, in addition to satisfying our need for seeking certainty and usefulness, educational research should also be used to explore 'alternate (sometimes even conflicting) interpretations of the phenomena under scrutiny' (p. 24). Arts-based research has merits towards achieving both goals.

Following this line of argument, I propose criteria for assessing the rigour of arts-based research, and researchers can self-assess their research design using the following questions.

DOI: 10.4324/9781003196105-4

First, does the research design successfully evoke thoughts, feelings, and experiences that were previously unintelligible or unconscious to the research participant? Arts are explorative in nature. When performing poetry, plays, visual arts or music, research participants can engage with a much wider spectrum of sensational experiences related to the educational phenomena. The role of the researcher is to help the research participants to co-create artworks that broaden their ways of knowing (Smithbell, 2010). The boundaries of rational thinking can be broken free. Imagination and individualised interpretation are allowed. Data can be presented in alternative forms other than numbers or words.

Second, does the art-creation process provide research participants with a vantage point to re-examine or re-imagine the fossilised theories and practices in education? A good piece of arts-based research should encourage critiquing theories and practices that have been taken for granted. This is achieved by researchers inviting participants not to represent reality but to recreate it. For instance, by asking the question 'can classroom teaching be conducted in artistic forms other than lecturing', educators have creatively incorporated drama, music, storytelling, drawing, dancing, and so on to enrich the traditional pedagogy (Bagley & Castro-Salazar, 2012; Smithbell, 2010).

In addition to enriching perceptions and expressions, arts-based research can also be used to reflect on and even replace the researcher's deeply rooted central position on data collection. Siegesmund (2014) called this function of arts-based research perpetuating provoking. For example, in a recent cross-national study on father–child interactions, researchers gave young children digital cameras to record conflicts with their fathers (Chawla-Duggan et al., 2020). In the data collection process, the children chose the moments of conflicts to record (visual reflexivity) and then provided their narratives (dialect reflexivity) about them in an interview with the researcher. The whole study relied on children's dialectic and visual reflexivity and deliberately weakened researchers' dominant role in the research. Chawla-Duggan et al. (2020) found that this arts-based research method can better enable research participants to speak from their own perspective and in their own voice.

Third, does the art-based research design empower research participants to voice unique experiences or to challenge the dominant discourses in education? This is related to the previous point, that arts-based research should be rooted in critiquing reality and proposing changes. Unlike most mainstream research methods, arts-based research gives researchers more liberty to explore alternative reality through metaphors and embodied experiences. As Barone (2001), citing Baldwin (1962, p. 16), put it, good art has the power to 'lay bare questions that have been hidden by the answers' (p. 16). It is interesting to note that most research designs, methods and questions, and even scholars' voices, have today become more 'standardised', so that they adhere to scientific journals' publication guidelines and fit into mainstream academic culture. For example, the past two decades have witnessed a large number of publications that explore the correlations and sometimes the causality between standardised test results and education policies, teacher performance, and school leadership. Thanks to the open-access standardised test and survey datasets from PISA and TALIS, similar statistical analyses can be easily duplicated to yield country-specific reports as well as international comparative studies. According to Mayer (2000), these studies are deemed more scientific, as they come with precise numbers and figures that can be used to guide practices. Without denying the value and importance of these studies, scholars who endorse arts-based research methods also want to protect the space in which personal, cultural, and unique experiences that deviate from mainstream discourses can be captured and expressed in our scientific world.

Fourth, does the research design create a plausible and credible artistic environment that attracts research participants to engage in the study? Barone (2001) suggests that researchers can create a virtual world for the research purpose, but it has to incorporate features of the real world that are relatable to the participants. Furthermore, the narrative drive, visual stimuli, fictional characters, and sequencing of events can be artistically orchestrated to evoke feelings and experiences beyond the constraints of everyday life. A rigorous arts-based research project should be able to entice participants, and later the reader, into an interrogation of the real world (Given, 2008).

Eisner (2017, p. 101) uses the term 'consensual validation' to describe attaining agreement on the interpretation of a phenomenon being as valid as securing authentication for its description. Seeking isomorphism in arts-based research is futile because individual participants describe and present their understanding of a phenomenon in myriad artistic forms. Notably, the consensus here is achieved by the reader resonating with participants' artistic expressions and interpretations of the lived experience and does not refer to agreement among the research participants. When participating in educational research, teachers, school leaders, students, and parents may share similar experiences, but their artistic expressions of such experiences can differ. Sometimes these participants' experiences do not overlap because they connect to different dimensions of an event. As researchers, we do not expect such participants to reach consensus. Our goal is to inform readers that these artistic expressions of viewpoints are embodied in the viewers, who hold different perspectives. Therefore, readers should have these different orientations in mind when interpreting research findings. A rigorous study should be able to evoke resonance among readers and provoke them to re-examine their own educational practices.

ENABLES project

Arts-based educational research utilises a wide range of data, such as artwork (e.g. collage, drama, music, poetry, or dance), interviews, observations, documents, and occasionally quantitative surveys to understand a studied phenomenon. Scholars in the European Arts-Based Development of Distributed Leadership and Innovation in Schools (ENABLES) project collected data such as gesture responses and participants' writing prompted by research questions (Woods et al., 2021). As discussed in the previous chapter, multiple types of data may support, supplement, or contradict the interpretation and evaluation of the studied phenomenon. The purpose of using multiple types of data is beyond triangulation. Through data analysis, researchers look for plausible conclusions from cogent narratives, incisive observations, and logical reasoning (Eisner, 2017).

Depending on the research purpose and design, researchers can devise their own framework for analysing data. Taking the analytical framework used in the ENABLES project as an example, Woods et al. (2021) examined evidence of change from the collage data, interview data, prompted writings, and gesture responses. Because they adopted the action research design and the purpose of the study was to use arts-based methods to develop distributed leadership and innovation in schools, they comprehensively analysed the data using the following five categories and sub-categories: *Change in aesthetic quality* (A1 affective attributes, A2 aesthetic awareness, A3 aesthetic reflexivity, A4 self-orientated awareness, A5 other-orientated awareness), *View of leadership, Capabilities of collaborative leadership and practice* (C1 capacity for proactive leadership, C2 status adaptability, C3 communicative virtues, C4 relational capabilities, C5 reciprocal leadership learning), *Practice* (P1 actual, P2 intentional), and *Other* (Woods et al., 2021, pp. 29–30).

Woods et al. (2021) highlight that new educational leadership knowledge, awareness, and capabilities are developed in a collaborative learning environment, and arts-based research can provide this embodied learning process. Echoing my previous point that arts-based educational research aims to interrogate taken-for-granted daily practices and theory and to create alternative ways of seeing the world, Woods et al. (2021) believe that research participants should open up to 'the affective and creative aspects' of themselves and others as well as to 'the interrelationship of cognitive and bodily experience' (p. 9). Following these underlying principles of arts-based research, their analytical framework rightfully puts the focus on change and relations (using words such as collaborative, communicative, reciprocal, and relational).

It is worth noting that during their data analysis, Woods et al. (2021) further refined their conceptualisation of practice in the framework. They recognised that 'changes in feelings, awareness and cognitive and embodied knowledge imbue practice' and that reflection 'is part of practice, not a separate variable impacting upon practice' (pp. 77–78). From this example of an analytical framework, we can see that arts-based research follows a spiral process through which data analysis, interpretation, and evaluation feedback to and change researchers' previous understanding.

Project on distributed leadership in Finnish and Chinese schools

In the next section of this chapter, I use my own study as an example to illustrate part of the data analysis procedure. The data used for analysis include individual participants' demographic information (i.e. pseudonyms, country, role in the school and gender), photographs of individually made collages, brief descriptions of the collages, and interview transcripts. To protect anonymity, I have given pseudonyms to the research participants and their schools (Allen, 2017). Original interview audio records and participants' informed consent forms, which could potentially reveal their identities, were safely stored in a password-protected hard drive. I alone had access to these during the research project, and the original files were destroyed 24 months after the completion of the project.

In this research project, participants from both Finnish and Chinese schools were invited to make collages that expressed their personal understanding of the school leadership structure and distribution within the school. The participants were told that there were no right or wrong answers. They could use any materials or draw pictures on a piece of blank A4 paper for the collages, but no written words were allowed. After completing their collages, each participant attended a semi-structured interview to explain their artwork's meaning and their lived experiences of leadership at the school. Table 4.1 shows examples of the collages and the follow-up interviews with four participants. Due to the word limit of this book, I only extracted part of the interviews for illustration purposes.

Table 4.1 Examples of collages and interview transcripts.

Participant	Photograph of the collage	Description of the collage	Interview transcript (part)
Matti (Pseudonym) Finland (LF1) Lower secondary school principal Male	*Figure 4.1* Collage made by LF1. Source: Photograph by the author.	This collage consists of seven pieces of coloured paper in circular form, each with an orange heart at its centre. A gold circle is positioned slightly above six other circles. There is gold thread connecting the gold circle to the others. Some smaller flowers and pink hearts are spread across the collage.	Matti: I wanted to use different colours and shapes, just like the others. The gold circle is the principal, who is above others. The other circles are the six teams we have in the school. I believe that every team leader has a heart, and everyone wants to do their best. However, sometimes the reality does not always match our expectations, so we have to do things in different ways. The gold thread means that we have a lot of responsibilities. We bear responsibility for the school's finances as well as teaching and learning; we are accountable to the educational authorities and the parents, etc. These flowers are the teachers in our school. Actually, I did not put the students here. I have the feeling that everyone wants to do their best, and that's why I chose bright colours. Well, in reality, we are different people, and even though we all have good intentions, we sometimes do things in different ways. This may make things look a bit messy in school. The pink hearts are the other staff, such as the teaching assistants, in our school. I think our teachers always want to do their best, even when the situation is sometimes quite challenging. Q: Do the teams have overlapping areas of responsibility? Matti: Yes, their responsibilities overlap. Q: Where do you see yourself? Matti: As one of the team members. But the principal is the gold circle above the others; as the principal has to be responsible for everything in school. Others do not bear the same responsibilities. But we all want to support the principal, and everyone is connected to the principal.

(*Continued*)

38 Research rigour and data collection

Table 4.1 (Continued)

Participant	Photograph of the collage	Description of the collage	Interview transcript (part)
Anni (Pseudonym) Finland (TF1) Lower secondary school home economics teacher Female	*Figure 4.2* Collage made by TF1. Source: Photograph by the author.	This collage has a wooden lid in the middle with a little pink heart on top of it. There are coloured stars surrounding the wooden lid. Beneath the stars, coloured feathers can be found at the bottom of the collage. On top of the feathers, there are coloured cocktail sticks, with some spikes pointing towards the stars, while others are pointing outwards.	Q: Is there any horizontal collaboration among the teams? Matti: Not much. The paper is a bit too small. I wanted to put all the six teams on the same level. Then, they all have a direction connection with the principal. Anni: My work looks like a 5-year-old's work. Hahaha . . . But I like it. The colourful feathers are the pupils. They are very light and can be blown away by the wind. The grey background here means that in some schools, students are seen as a grey mass; everyone is the same. But this is not the case in our school. Here, every pupil is seen as an individual with his or her own personality. I think our principal also sees our pupils as individuals. How the principal thinks about the students is very important. This means our school respects every human being. These sticks are parents. Sometimes, parents can be a bit aggressive. Hahaha . . . That's why I put some of the forks upwards. But they are also individuals, and we collaborate (with parents) a lot. The stars are the teachers because we are the real stars, although we do not always say it aloud. We do not have a specific place to be; we are everywhere. Sometimes teachers encounter things in their private life, so they can be a bit trapped in a corner. Sometimes teachers spend more time with the students, so they are more closely linked to the pupils. Teachers can switch positions in my picture, but we are mostly with our pupils. This is our principal. He is the wooden part, like a tree. He is always

there. I can always turn to him to ask whatever questions I have. He has a good heart. In our school, we can freely express our opinions. To me, the principal is not at the top but in the middle, among us. Maybe he is the heart of the school. Of course, the pupils are the core of the school, but I think the principal is the heart of the school. Of course, our principal has authority, but he is willing to talk to us. He wants to know how we are doing, and that makes him the heart of the school.

Q: I like that. You see the school as a very lively community.
Anni: Yes. You will come to see our Independence Day celebration tomorrow; then you will see what our pupils are doing together. They could do that if we did not have this culture. We do things together, and whatever we do, we ask our principal. He will think about it and then say it is ok. He always thinks about what the pupils want. For him, he thinks that having the Independence Day celebration is what the pupils want, and that's why we are having it: to have some fun in school. Everyone is different. It may lead to a mess, but it is not a mess.

Q: Do you think the school leadership is quite spread around, among different people?
Anni: Yes, I think so. But at the same time, it is also important to have the wood (the principal) here so we know he is the one we can trust and rely on. But I did not put the vice-principals in this picture. They are also teachers, of course; they could be next to the principal as well.

(Continued)

Table 4.1 (Continued)

Participant	Photograph of the collage	Description of the collage	Interview transcript (part)
Feng (Pseudonym) China (LC1) Upper secondary school principal Male	*Figure 4.3* Collage made by LC1. Photograph by the author.	The whole collage resembles a cross. Feng put a picture of the Eiffel Tower on the top. In the middle, there is a picture of a scooter. To its left, Feng placed a picture of Venice in which two boats, a canal and some buildings are presented. To its right, there are pictures of a clock and a coffee cup. Above these is placed a small crown. Beneath the scooter picture, Feng put a picture of the Arc de Triomphe. All these pictures are connected by paper strips. In addition to the pictures that form a cross, two-coloured balloons are placed diagonally on the paper.	Feng: This is my school leadership model. It starts with a tower on the top, which means having an all-round vision. The Arc de Triomphe at the bottom symbolises achievement. From the Eiffel tower to the Arc de Triomphe, we need actions. So, you can see the scooter picture here. We also need collective effort (pointing at the boats to the left). These two pictures mean we have to focus on practice and taking actions in the school. On the right-hand side, the clock shows the importance of time management. The coffee cup underlines the importance of interpersonal communication. The little crown above the coffee cup signifies motivation. Sometimes we have to motivate others by crowning them with a tall hat (in Chinese: 戴高帽子 means flattering or praising someone). Only when all these factors work together in the school can we walk towards the Arc de Triomphe. Q: Where do you see yourself in the collage? Feng: I am the school principal, so I see myself in every picture. I envision the future of the school and constantly persuade people that we can realise the vision. In the school management process, I play different roles. Sometimes I am a servant and a motivator; sometimes I am an action-taker and a supervisor. I am in the entire process from goal-setting to goal achievement. Q: Why did you put the two balloons in the collage? Feng: They refer to our colourful campus activities. Because teaching and learning is hard work, we should also add fun to school life. School should be a home for everyone.

Tang (Pseudonym) (TC1) China Lower secondary Chinese language teacher Female	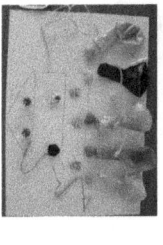 *Figure 4.4* Collage made by TC1. Source: Photograph by the author.	The whole collage resembles a pyramid. Tang drew a triangle and placed two crowns into it to form the first tier of the hierarchy. Underneath that, she drew a rectangle and placed inside it one black camellia flower and a silver heart-shaped stone. Beneath the second tier, Tang drew a trapezium and placed three bear-shaped buttons inside it. Beneath them are five-coloured heart-shaped buttons, below which are five-coloured balloons. On the picture, there are three ribbons, one laid above the balloons on the lowest level and the other two placed alongside the three-tier pyramid.	Tang: I made this collage based on my feelings. Every school has a centralised administrative system in which the most important leadership comes from the principal and the Communist Party branch secretary. So, I put two crowns on the top of the pyramid. Below the two crowns, there are two implementors, who are our vice-principals. They take charge of moral education and pedagogy, respectively. I used the black camellia flower to symbolise our female moral education vice-principal, who exercises feminine leadership. In contrast, the vice-principal in charge of pedagogy demonstrates divergent thinking. I wanted to use a five-pointed star to symbolise him, but this silver heart-shaped stone will do as well. It is shiny, which means the vice-principal looks for the strengths in every teacher. At the same time, the vice-principal delegates teaching tasks every year. I think this heart signifies that pedagogical leadership requires a leader to put his heart into work. Beneath the two vice-principals, the three bears are practitioners. They are the directors of the Department of Academic Affairs, the Department of Student Affairs and the Principal's Office. They work directly with teachers in each year group and subject group. Underneath the bears, we have many colourful hearts. They are the subject leaders and the year-group leaders. On the lowest level are our teachers. They are under different levels of leaders. Therefore, teachers have pressure and motivation. They have to be flexible and elastic; just like the balloons, there is no fixed shape. Our teachers show different shapes in different situations.

(*Continued*)

Table 4.1 (Continued)

Participant	Photograph of the collage	Description of the collage	Interview transcript (part)
			Q: You also put some ribbons on the picture. What do they mean? Tang: They symbolise communication, both vertically between teachers and leaders and horizontally between leaders and between teachers. School is a centralised administrative organisation, but it is different from government. Every school has its culture, and that power of culture cannot be overlooked. Teachers influence each other. From bottom up, teachers express their opinions, and then there is the top-down implementation of some of the teachers' ideas. These ribbons mean we have communication across various levels.

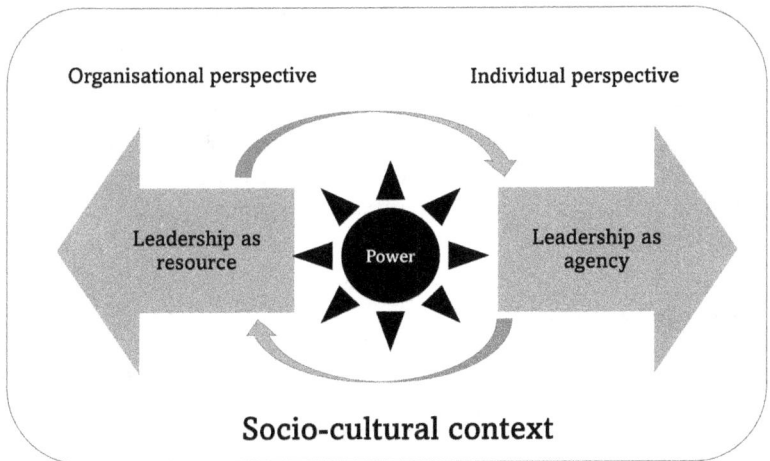

Figure 4.5 Resource–agency duality model of distributed leadership (Tian, 2016, p. 18)

When analysing the data, I applied the resource–agency duality model of distributed leadership (Tian, 2016). Guided by the model (Figure 4.5), I looked for collage elements as well as narratives that depicted participants' views on the following seven dimensions of distributed leadership:

- their school's sociocultural context;
- organisational resources distributed to various school members;
- agency used by school members to influence others or decision-making;
- the participant's position in the collage and their relationship with others;
- the directions of power;
- critical incidents where power conflict or tension took place;
- the participant's feelings and emotions about school leadership and this research project.

This is the analytical framework from Tian's (2016) distributed leadership study. The rectangular box means the school socio-cultural context, within which there are two arrows pointing to the opposite directions. One arrow refers to leadership as a resource from the organisational perspective and the other arrow refers to leadership as agency from the individual perspective. Resource and agency can convert into each other when they align or polarise when they misalign. Between the two arrows, there is power pointing at multiple directions.

Each collage and respective interview were paired for analysis. Coloured codes were used to highlight elements corresponding to each key dimension of distributed leadership in the analytical framework. The participants' roles were taken into consideration when analysing their perspectives of distributed leadership. For example, I was interested in uncovering whether principals' views of distributed leadership differed from those of teachers, students, and non-teaching staff; when describing the same incident, I wanted to know how their narratives and experiences diverged or converged, and why. Some findings from the study are reported in Chapter 5.

Things to be considered

It is worth mentioning that when collecting the data, I had a school senior leadership team in one group and teachers, students, and non-teaching staff in their own groups. This helped the participants freely express their ideas without worrying about the presence of their superiors/staff. On two occasions, individual teachers wanted to have a one-on-one interview with me, instead of participating in the focus group interview, because they wanted to share some sensitive topics about power conflicts and criticisms on school leadership. I accepted their request and created an emotionally safe environment with blinds and soundproof windows to ensure their anonymity and privacy. All the participants were given ten calendar days to decide if they wanted to withdraw from the study after the collage-making and interview in case they felt uncomfortable about sharing their personal experiences and feelings. No participants withdrew in this particular project. However, it is imperative for educational researchers to offer and articulate this right to participants in the Informed Consent Form (see Figure 3.3 in Chapter 3) as well as at the beginning of the data collection.

In Chapter 5, I explain how to report findings from arts-based research projects.

References

Allen, M. (2017). *The SAGE encyclopedia of communication research methods*. SAGE Publications, Inc. https://doi.org/10.4135/9781483381411

Bagley, C., & Castro-Salazar, R. (2012). Critical arts-based research in education: Performing undocumented historias. *British Educational Research Journal*, *38*(2), 239–260. https://doi.org/10.1080/01411926.2010.538667

Baldwin, J. (1962). *The creative process*. Ridge Press. https://openspaceofdemocracy.files.wordpress.com/2017/01/baldwin-creative-process.pdf

Barone, T. (2001). Science, art, and the predispositions of educational researchers. *Educational Researcher*, *30*(7), 24–28. https://doi.org/10.3102/0013189X030007024

Chawla-Duggan, R., Konantambigi, R., Lam, M. M. S., & Sollied, S. (2020). A visual methods approach for researching children's perspectives: Capturing the dialectic and visual reflexivity in a cross-national study of father-child interactions. *International Journal of Social Research Methodology*, *23*(1), 37–54. https://doi.org/10.1080/13645579.2019.1672283

Eisner, E. W. (2017). *The enlightened eye: Qualitative inquiry and the enhancement of educational practice*. Teachers College Press.

Given, L. (Ed.). (2008). *The SAGE encyclopedia of qualitative research methods: Vols. 1–0*. SAGE Publications, Inc. https://doi.org/10.4135/9781412963909

Mayer, R. E. (2000). What is the place of science in educational research? *Educational Researcher*, *29*(6), 38–39.

Siegesmund, R. (2014). The N of 1 in arts-based research: Reliability and validity. *International Journal of Education & the Arts*, *15*(2.5), 1–13.

Smithbell, P. (2010). Arts-based research in education: A review. *The Qualitative Report*, *15*(6), 1597–1601.

Tian, M. (2016). Distributed leadership in Finnish and Shanghai schools. *Jyväskylä Studies in Education, Psychology and Social Research*, *571*. https://jyx.jyu.fi/dspace/handle/123456789/52197

Woods, P. A., Culshaw, S., Jarvis, J., Payne, H., Roberts, A., & Smith, K. (2021). *Developing distributed leadership through arts-based and embodied methods: An evaluation of the UK action research trials of collage and gesture response* (The European Arts-Based Development of Distributed Leadership and Innovation in Schools (ENABLES) Project). Centre for Educational Leadership, School of Education, University of Hertfordshire. www.herts.ac.uk/__data/assets/pdf_file/0020/340913/4.B.1_Collage-and-gesture_ARTs-report.pdf

5 Reporting, interpreting, and discussing findings

Reporting findings

After collecting and analysing their data, researchers move on to the phase involving reporting the findings. As illustrated in the previous chapter, arts-based research projects generate multiple types of data, such as pictures, narratives, audios, videos, and artefacts. Through the collage-making example I presented in Chapter 4, the research participants had an immersive experience. They were able to cut, manoeuvre, and assemble art materials to make a collage that expressed their lived experiences of school leadership. The artworks were photographed by the researcher. After that, each participant was interviewed about the meaning of their collage as well as the collage-making process. By doing so, the participants 'transitioned in and out of the intersubjective arts-space, experienced the challenges of creating arts-based responses within the intersubjective space' (Gerber et al., 2018, p. 4). The multiple types of data were coded separately to generate formative findings. After that, a summative hybrid synthesis was conducted to draw connections across the findings.

Table 5.1 shows one example of formative findings drawn from four collages reported in Table 4.1 in Chapter 4. Using the units of analysis, leadership structure, choice of colour and artefacts, and leadership boundaries, I compared and contrasted the distribution of leadership embedded in the four collages.

If we only look at this small sample of four collages, there are no clear distinctions between the principals' (LF1 and LC1) and the teachers' (TF1 and TC1) views on leadership distribution. Neither can we detect clear disparities in leadership distribution in Finnish and Chinese schools. However, if we examine all the 112 collages collected from the four groups of participants (i.e. senior leaders, teachers, students, and non-teaching staff) in three Finnish and five Chinese schools, some interesting patterns of distributed leadership emerged from this research project.

Table 5.1 Example of formative findings based on collages

Unit of analysis	LF1, TF1, and TC1 all used art materials to visualise leaders (e.g. hearts, wood lid, flowers, and crowns), teachers (e.g. stars and balloons), students (e.g. feathers), and parents (e.g. cocktail picks). The unit of analysis was people.
	LC1 used symbolic pictures (e.g. Arc de Triomphe, clock, Eiffel Tower, and boats) to illustrate key leadership practices (e.g. achievement, time pressure, action, and collective agency). The unit of analysis was leadership practice.
Leadership structure	LF1 and TC1 visualised a top-down pyramid school leadership structure. TF1 depicted a spider's web structure with the school principal in the middle of the network. LC1 described the leader as part of every process in the school's machinery and did not have a fixed position in the collage.
Choice of colour and artefacts	Between-group diversity was shown in the way that all the research participants used different colours and artefacts to illustrate different roles and types of leadership work in the school. In the collages of LF1, TF1, and TC1, the within-group similarity was manifested in the choice of the same artefacts (e.g. stars as teachers, feathers as students, crowns as top leaders, and bears as middle leaders).
Leadership boundaries	LF1, LC1, and TC1's collages showed how leadership affected school leaders, teachers, and students on the school campus. TF1's view on leadership also extended to the interaction between home and school.

For example, the non-teaching staff, including school secretaries, librarians, administrators, and school nurses, tended to view leadership as flowing from the top to the bottom. To them, leadership was first and foremost position-based. Interestingly, they also appeared to exclude themselves from the collages, suggesting they did not view non-teaching staff as part of the leadership structure or empowered leaders. Some visualised themselves as loosely associated school members because they worked for several schools in the district. The only exception was two school secretaries who visualised their personal work relationship with the principals in their collages. On an interpersonal level, the principal exercised formal leadership over the teachers, while the secretary exercised informal leadership by influencing the principal's agenda, passing on information, and coordinating with external stakeholders such as the local community and other schools.

In terms of the students' views, most of them used a triangle shape to illustrate a leadership structure consisting of senior school leaders at the top, subject leaders in the middle, and teachers at the bottom. None of the students from either the Chinese or Finnish schools included parents or non-teaching staff in their collages. In a few collages, the students used a few artefacts to symbolise student leaders, while most students without school-level leadership roles were not visible in the picture. One Finnish student drew pictures of three teachers whom he saw as role models. According to this particular collage, leadership was perceived on an interpersonal level and in the format of teachers' moral leadership.

Previous studies have suggested that Chinese schools tend to adopt a more hierarchical structure with a high power distance between the top leader and the grassroots teachers. In contrast, Finnish schools are more egalitarian, with a low power distance (Brunila et al., 2017; Bryant & Rao, 2019; Chen & Tjosvold, 2007; Heikka & Suhonen, 2019; Zheng et al., 2019). One would assume that school leaders and teachers in the two countries visualise leadership structures and distributions in similar ways when creating collages. Interestingly, that was not the case in my study. Leaders and teachers from both contexts visualised leadership in a variety of ways. Some collages resembled a hierarchical pyramid structure, some showed a matrix structure, some were in the format of networks, and some adopted a horizontal structure. The collage data also challenged one previous finding, that the principals tend to perceive a lower power distance between the leadership team and the teachers than what is experienced from the teachers' point of view. In other words, principals think that they are more approachable compared with how the teachers view them. At least according to the collage data collected in my project, there was no evidence confirming that visualised power distance between the leaders and the teachers correlated with the roles of the collage-makers.

After analysing the collage data, I moved on to analysing and reporting the follow-up interviews. The example I have provided in Table 4.1 shows interview excerpts after the collage-making. These interviews brought more nuances to the meanings of the collages. With the visual aids (i.e. artefacts used in the collages and their relationships), the research participants felt that they were able to review the existing leadership structures and distributions through a critical lens.

For instance, according to TC1:

> On the lowest level are our teachers. They are under different levels of leaders. Therefore, teachers are under pressure and motivated. They have to be flexible and elastic. Just like the balloons, there is no fixed shape. Our teachers have different shapes in different situations.

This narrative seemed to suggest that teachers in that school had little agency in terms of decision-making and were only led by multiple layers of leadership. However, the teachers were able to respond to various situations in different ways, which demonstrated agency. This agency could be active, such as by implementing decisions, or negative, such as by resisting or ignoring the leadership. When describing her collage-making experience, TC1 later explained that the process had made her reflect on the status quo. After answering a question about how leadership was distributed in the school, she naturally wondered if leadership should be distributed in this way, and how could she, as a teacher, make a contribution to the leadership work. She declared that she would not have considered these questions were it not for her participating in the collage-making.

As I mentioned earlier, if we looked solely at the collage data, there would not be any distinctive patterns that differentiated the Finnish school leaders and teachers' views on leadership from those of their counterparts in the Chinese schools. However, the follow-up interviews unearthed two special features shared by the Finnish school leaders and teachers. One was the way that they visualised and talked about power tensions and conflicts in the school.

In his interview, LF1 mentioned:

> Well, in reality, we are different people, and even if we all have good intentions, we sometimes do things in different ways. This may make things look a bit messy in school.

Similar narratives could be found in a number of other interviews with the Finnish school leaders and teachers. Small interest groups, information gatekeepers, and lobbyists were visualised in the collages. Some interviewees mentioned the power conflicts they had experienced or witnessed in the school. When scarce resources failed to meet everyone's needs, leadership decisions were often influenced by opinion leaders or lobbyists in subtle ways. As the resource–agency duality model of distributed leadership (Figure 4.5) illustrated, when organisational resources misalign with individual's agency, power tensions and conflicts start to pull people towards different directions.

The Chinese school leaders and teachers, by contrast, tended to perceive interest groups receiving certain favours from the leader as part of their visionary leadership, rather than as micropolitical conflicts. For example, in one Chinese school, the principal gave two teachers exclusive continuing professional development opportunities 1 year ahead of time and made them the only eligible candidates for leadership roles in a teacher leader election organised by the school. Both the principal and a few teachers in that school described this case as the leader recognising and enabling the teachers' leadership potential. Social injustice and power abuse were not flagged as issues in either the collages or the interviews. These culturally nuanced understandings of distributed leadership are illuminated by arts-based methods.

The other key cultural difference that the interviewees discerned was the blurred boundaries between leaders and followers in Finnish schools. The interviewees mentioned that many Finnish schools rotated leadership responsibilities among teachers instead of providing a rigid career progression pipeline, as was often found in the Chinese schools. This explained why many Finnish leaders and teachers perceived leadership as a form of service rather than power. They recognised the leadership process to be 'messy', 'difficult' and 'tricky'. How leadership emerged from continued negotiations, debates, and even conflicts was more evident in the Finnish schools. Some interviewees mentioned that they had become more aware of these hidden micropolitics when engaging with collage making. The tangible artefacts stimulated their memories. Lived experiences flashed through their minds and simultaneously evoked feelings. The whole process enabled them to better articulate their understanding of school leadership through details of lived experiences, rather than through abstract concepts.

From the above examples of the research findings, I hope that readers can gain some ideas of how first to report formative findings generated from different datasets, such as collage data and interview data, and then to dissect how the art-making process stimulates participants' reflections and re-imagination on the topic. In the following section, I explain how to interpret and discuss findings.

Interpreting and discussing findings

Because arts-based research projects are often designed in a mixed-method, multi-layered, and non-linear way, it is imperative that researchers learn to sit comfortably with the diverse non-conclusive findings generated from such studies. Polarised views should be honestly reported as much as shared understandings of a topic. I would reiterate here that the purpose of arts-based research is not to distil data into a handful of conclusions but to present a plethora of perceptions and lived experiences meaningful to the individuals (Cahnmann-Taylor & Siegesmund, 2018). When interpreting and discussing findings, it is essential to explain how the art-making process has enabled research participants to acquire new perspectives, feel empowered, and build connections with others (Ball et al., 2021). This special power of arts-based research methods can provide a valuable contribution to the existing knowledge base.

In the ENABLES project, for example, Woods et al. (2021) found that collages and gesture responses can effectively open up possibilities for the research participants to re-examine their views of leadership and relationships with others. According to their analysis, the relational aspect of leadership was embedded in one collage as giving someone a hand up. By creating this image, the participant changed her understanding of leadership from doing things correctly to supporting others (Woods et al., 2021). This transformation was honestly recorded by the research team in their project report.

I largely share this sentiment of arts-based research methods as a means for transformation. This is closely linked to Denzin's (1971) logic of naturalistic inquiry, through which researchers can theorise a complex world from people's behaviours, languages, attitudes, and feelings as well as the environment that shapes them. It is the inductive approach, rather than the deductive method, that allows researchers to explore the subjective and cultural dimensions of a studied social phenomenon (Giddens, 2013). Research participants are given a voice to speak for themselves. The traditional hypothetico-deductive methodology gives researchers a privileged status because they can choose a theory, generate hypotheses and form questions to test these hypotheses (Thorpe & Holt, 2008). Under this framework, research participants' answers are largely confined to the parameters predetermined by researchers. Arts-based methods as an inductive methodology liberates research participants' knowledge and imagination. They open up new avenues for discussion and contribute to existing knowledge (Hanzalik, 2021).

Inductive and deductive methods are not mutually exclusive but complementary (Butler-Kisber, 2008). In my own research project, presented earlier, the findings from the collage-making workshops and interviews brought new insights into distributed leadership knowledge in the following ways. First, non-teaching staff and students were included in the research project. These groups have been largely understudied in distributed leadership research. Their marginalised position in school leadership work was, to a large extent, internalised, which was shown in their collages and narratives. Most non-teaching staff and students did not picture themselves as part of the leadership structure, or they depicted themselves as the recipients of others' leadership. By participating in the arts-based research project, some of them started to reflect on their marginalised position and looked for potential leadership resources (e.g. student union, trade union, or school forum) accessible to them.

The second contribution from this arts-based research project is providing novel perspectives to understand Finnish and Chinese school leadership. The difference of power distance was manifested in the way the school leaders and teachers talked about power conflicts and tensions. It appears that many Finnish schools would rotate leadership responsibilities among the teachers. This flexible leadership structure enabled more teachers to access leadership resources and exercise their agency through lobbying and networking. In this research project, Finish school leaders and teachers talked openly about messy decision-making as a result of various interest groups exercising formal and informal power. Chinese teachers, by contrast, tended to perceive micropolitics as a form of formal leadership. If a leader distributed more resources to favourable teachers or acquiesced in this decision, it was not directly challenged by other teachers for the reasons of institutional injustice or unfairness but perceived as part of the leader's visionary leadership. Hence, in Chinese schools, teachers consider the top leaders first and foremost as a leadership resource because it is this type of blended interpersonal and professional relationship that determines one's career advancement. When different types of power relations are unpacked in collages and interviews, a comparative study can offer more nuanced understandings of complex phenomena.

Lastly, arts-based research methods can inform and facilitate change. All the eight schools participating in this research project launched structural changes in the 3 years subsequent to it. Three schools received new principals, two elected new senior leadership teams, two created matrix structures to allow both vertical and horizontal collaboration, and one received a new principal and later removed one layer of middle leadership to enhance communication and efficiency. I would not be so bold as to claim that all these changes were the result of participation in the research project. However, a number of research participants, both school leaders and teachers, reached out to me after the project to say that the collage-making workshops had helped them to reflect on resource distribution and to reconstruct teams. After that, I started to realise the power of arts-based research on practice. It does not stop at uncovering 'what distributed leadership is' in practice but goes two steps further by asking 'what distributed leadership can be' and 'how can we make that happen'. The first step is transformation, and the second and third steps are activism. In the following chapter, I examine the impact of arts-based research and some of the controversies surrounding this methodology.

References

Ball, S., Leach, B., Bousfield, J., Smith, P., & Marjanovic, S. (2021). *Arts-based approaches to public engagement with research: Lessons from a rapid review* (p. 111). RAND Corporation.

Brunila, K., Ikävalko, E., Kurki, T., Masoud, A., Mertanen, K., Mikkola, A., & Mäkelä, K. (2017). Transitions, justice, and equity in education in Finland. *Oxford Encyclopedia of Education*. http://education.oxfordre.com/view/10.1093/acrefore/9780190264093.001.0001/acrefore-9780190264093-e-130

Bryant, D. A., & Rao, C. (2019). Teachers as reform leaders in Chinese schools. *International Journal of Educational Management*, 33(4), 663–677. ERIC.

Butler-Kisber, L. (2008). Collage as inquiry. In J. Knowles & A. Cole (Eds.), *Handbook of the arts in qualitative research: Perspectives, methodologies, examples, and issues* (pp. 265–277). SAGE Publications, Inc. https://doi.org/10.4135/9781452226545.n22

Cahnmann-Taylor, M., & Siegesmund, R. (2018). *Arts-based research in education: Foundations for practice* (2nd ed.). Routledge.

Chen, N. Y.-F., & Tjosvold, D. (2007). Guanxi and leader member relationships between American managers and Chinese employees: Open-minded dialogue as mediator. *Asia Pacific Journal of Management, 24*(2), 171–189. https://doi.org/10.1007/s10490-006-9029-9

Denzin, N. K. (1971). The logic of naturalistic inquiry. *Social Forces, 50*(2), 166–182. https://doi.org/10.2307/2576935

Gerber, N., Bryl, K., Potvin, N., & Blank, C. A. (2018). Arts-based research approaches to studying mechanisms of change in the creative arts therapies. *Frontiers in Psychology, 9*. www.frontiersin.org/articles/10.3389/fpsyg.2018.02076

Giddens, A. (2013). *New rules of sociological method: A positive critique of interpretative sociologies* (2nd ed.). John Wiley & Sons.

Hanzalik, K. (2021). *Arts-based research methods in writing studies: A primer*. Routledge. https://doi.org/10.4324/9781003099444

Heikka, J., & Suhonen, K. (2019). Distributed pedagogical leadership functions in early childhood education settings in Finland. *Southeast Asia Early Childhood, 8*(2), 43–56. ERIC.

Thorpe, R., & Holt, R. (2008). *The SAGE dictionary of qualitative management research*. SAGE Publications Ltd. https://doi.org/10.4135/9780857020109

Woods, P. A., Culshaw, S., Jarvis, J., Payne, H., Roberts, A., & Smith, K. (2021). *Developing distributed leadership through arts-based and embodied methods: An evaluation of the UK action research trials of collage and gesture response*. University of Hertfordshire. www.herts.ac.uk/__data/assets/pdf_file/0020/340913/4.B.1_Collage-and-gesture_ARTs-report.pdf

Zheng, X., Yin, H., & Liu, Y. (2019). The relationship between distributed leadership and teacher efficacy in China: The mediation of satisfaction and trust. *Asia-Pacific Education Researcher, 28*(6), 509–518.

6 Impact of arts-based research methods and controversies surrounding them

Using arts-based methods to enrich close-to-practice research

The British Educational Research Association published a report that pointed out that much educational research involves researchers collaborating with practitioners to solve problems in practice and to apply critical thinking in real-life scenarios (Wyse et al., 2017). Such close-to-practice research projects invite practitioners to define issues that are relevant and important to their daily practices and thus empower practitioners such as teaching professionals to collaborate with researchers and transform into educational researchers (Wyse et al., 2017). Many teaching professionals, such as arts, music, drama, and literature teachers, are already familiar with and use arts-based methods in their work. Hence, arts-based methods can enrich close-to-practice research and be used both as a form of enquiry and as pedagogy.

One close-to-practice study introduced street theatre as a form of critical pedagogy for teaching social studies in education (Datoo & Chagani, 2011). Compared with other forms of theatre, street theatre blurs the boundaries between spectators and actors. Performers set a scene featuring a particular socio-cultural political issue and invite spectators in the street to co-create the play via acting and creating dialogue. This arts-based method not only facilitates the audience's critical reflection on a real-life problem but also empowers them to act on it (Datoo & Chagani, 2011). The street theatre method can effectively empower groups such as immigrants and oppressed minorities to express their lived experiences in a contextualised social reality and, more importantly, to discover their agency in recreating these realities when playing roles in a spontaneous theatre (Darder et al., 2017). The study shows that the role play can, to some extent, alleviate personal and societal fears by creating an emotional safe space for empowered spectators/ actors to respond to their social realties (Datoo & Chagani, 2011). School

DOI: 10.4324/9781003196105-6

teachers, NGOs, and higher education institution lecturers may find this arts-based method useful as both a research method and a pedagogical tool when teaching complex topics such as equity, diversity, inclusion, racial inequality, and social injustice.

Poetry can be another powerful pedagogical and research tool for reaching audiences, evoking curiosity, and sparking the imagination that conventional academic prose falls short of doing (Fitzpatrick & Fitzpatrick, 2020). Faulkner (2019) highlighted that 'the power of poetic inquiry can be realised if we ride the dialectic between aesthetic and epistemic concerns' (p. 221). In educational research, some scholars believe that poetic inquiries can help them interrogate the neoliberal drive behind academic productivity and bring joy back to research. Hope-Gill (2020) raised an interesting point by arguing that poetry can soften the language of science. Between the aesthetic and epistemic terrains, arts-based methods give educational researchers a creative space to breathe, imagine, and capture the depth of human experience. For education professionals who conduct close-to-practice research, arts-based methods can offer them accessible and innovative tools to enrich their research projects.

Using arts-based methods to decolonise knowledge

In educational research, arts-based methods can empower educational leaders, teachers, and students from minority backgrounds to reframe dominant discourses on curricula and knowledge. For example, an ongoing curriculum decolonisation movement in UK higher education, *Why is My Curriculum White*, has challenged the overt and covert Eurocentric domination of university reading lists, lecture content, assignment formats, and assessment criteria. A White curriculum has been perpetuating a specific form of intellectual supremacy that has featured empiricism, rationality, and pragmatism since the Age of Enlightenment in Europe in the 17th century. A recent study has shown that elite universities in the UK and the USA tend to use their brands as a form of economic, social, and cultural capital to circulate dominant ideas that are produced by and serve a select few (Myers & Bhopal, 2021). Powerful knowledge was and continues to be produced by White scholars. In response to that, arts-based methods offer new tools to resist global knowledge politics and neoliberal knowledge production in higher education.

Arts-based methods, especially those derived from or familiar to marginalised and disadvantaged communities, such as theatre, visual arts, dance, poetry, and storytelling, can help everyone to reflect on the existing power relations and knowledge structure in education. Arts-based methods help us recognise minority groups' sociocultural capital and reclaim their narratives, which have been long neglected in our education systems (Hammond et al., 2018; Peters, 2015). For instance, Hammond et al.'s (2018, pp. 264–265) review shows that arts-based methods such as photovoice, drawing, and role-playing have been used in a South African study on gender equality and adult education (Daniels, 2002), digital storytelling, writing, collective stories, and photography have been used to teach education development, policy and cultural identity to the Inuit people of Nunavik, Canada (Garakani, 2014) and facilitated drawings have been used teach decolonisation and identity to a Dakota First Nation population in Canada (Yuen et al., 2013). In a study conducted in Columbia, arts-based research methods were employed to decolonise participatory methodologies. When working with Afro-Colombian and indigenous young people, Calderon et al. (2022) contended that it was not only powerful knowledge that educational researchers should decolonise but also the methodologies that they used to generate the powerful knowledge. Arts-based methods can, therefore, unleash the epistemic power embedded in indigenous knowledge to decolonise these methodologies.

Research participants from marginalised groups have found arts-based methods 'interesting and culturally relevant', and these methods can help them 'cultivate relationships of mutual trust, respect, and power' (Hammond et al., 2018, p. 268). Among these relationship-building activities, the relationship between the researcher and research participants is essential. Echoing Chapter 2 of this book, Hammond et al.'s (2018) literature review confirmed that arts-based research methods can effectively combat the 'colonial politics of research, in which researchers maintain a privileged position of knowledge production and interpretation' (p. 270). Arts-based research methods can also subvert this power imbalance and create a 'ceremony' of research in which all relationships are celebrated and nurtured (Wilson, 2008).

Using arts-based research to inform or change education policies

In addition to enriching close-to-practice research and decolonising knowledge, recent studies have shown that arts-based research can inform or change education policies. For example, digital media and arts-based methods have contributed to the European Commission's policy of promoting responsible research and innovation in science education (Ruiz-Mallén et al., 2021). More specifically, there is evidence to suggest that drama-based methods can facilitate the affective and embodied processing of scientific content and peer collaboration in science education. Digital tools such as video games and courseware provide new channels to develop students' problem-solving skills, while arts-based methods such as drama facilitate students' critical reflection on gender equality and ethical issues involved in science (Ruiz-Mallén et al., 2021).

Another example entails arts-based methods effectively challenging historic segregation policies and speaking up for minoritised groups that are most vulnerable to policies and cultures of oppression (Chappell & Cahnmann-Taylor, 2013). One study shows that within schools and local communities, artists work with researchers, teachers, students, and parents to reveal the impact of public policies on community members' daily lives. Documentaries, paintings, and creative writings vividly capture these cultural nuances and speak for minoritised groups who are often silenced in policy discourses. These arts-based methods also enable the majoritised group to re-examine their social dominance and privileges when they listen to alternative stories told by their minoritised counterparts (Schultz, 2008). In research and in education, the impact of arts-based methods has been recognised. Compared with traditional tools of inquiry, these methods have generated new evidence for formats that are more accessible and comprehensible to the public (Anyon, 2005). Looking to the future, policymakers can better utilise arts-based research methods and their findings to develop or revise education policies and give voice to subjugated perspectives to combat educational inequality and social injustice.

Controversies surrounding arts-based research methods

As discussed earlier, arts-based research methods can have a profound impact on close-to-practice research, knowledge decolonisation, and policymaking. However, Rice et al. (2021) also point out some potential risks involved in arts-based research. Because such research tends to evoke feelings that are intimate to the individuals, Boler (1997, 1999) and Butler (2004) flagged the risk of researchers and research participants owning other people's pain when using empathy during the research process. In order to understand someone else's lived experiences and to co-create knowledge, researchers and research participants often put themselves in the shoes of others to experience how they feel and assimilate what they embody. Empathy becomes a catalyst for identifying with another's position, making a moral judgement, and sometimes taking an action (Rice et al., 2021). This adds more shades of grey to research ethics. For instance, Goodley et al. (2018) warn us that in research, non-disabled people tend to become highly emotional when empathising with disabled people's stories. In the same vein, when using arts-based research to study racialised and gendered experiences of disadvantaged groups, powerful emotions triggered by empathy may, to some extent, distract participants from the social injustice issue itself (Boler, 1999; Rice et al., 2021). Other scholars, nevertheless, hold the opposite view. They believe that when suffering is consumed by a larger group, 'something of its horror [is] removed' (Cheng, 2004, p. 71; O'Neill et al., 2019). Some would even go so far as to say, because trust and relational good can emerge from this intertwined space of self and other, suffering-induced empathy is a key ingredient in arts-based research (O'Neill et al., 2019).

In this book, I argue that researchers should pay extra attention to the risks related to participants' emotional wellbeing when designing and conducting arts-based research. For instance, a debrief session can be organised after the data collection to discuss how empathy with others' experiences affect one's own private world and what drives one's actions for social change. Risk mitigation protocols should be explicitly presented to the research participants, including outlining their right to withdraw from the study if they feel emotionally distressed. Rice et al. (2021) propose a useful concept of 'difference-attuned empathy to refer to a practice of empathy that holds difference and ethical engagement at the heart of the connection' (pp. 350–351). This concept can assist research participants to discuss how to build a shared space for knowledge co-creation without eroding their own identities.

Another controversy involved in arts-based research is whether to judge the methods as well as the artworks on their truth value or on their aesthetic value. Here the aesthetic value does not mean that a piece of artwork is pleasing to the eye or triggers feelings of happiness; instead, it refers to if the arts-based method and the artwork can elicit deep reflection and alternative perspectives on the topic in question.

Taking the storytelling method as an example. What qualifies a good story in educational research? Mark Twain once said, 'Never let the truth get in the way of a good story.' Should the storytelling method allow a blurry line between fiction and reality? If so, how do we assess the research rigour? Can researchers discern any objective truth from a theatre play, a poem, or a painting? Should researchers judge the authenticity of contradictory testimonials in one story? If researchers judge an artwork on its truth value, do they risk decontextualising the lived experiences and presuming someone's version of truth is 'consumable, collapsible or destructible' (Rice et al., 2021, p. 356)? These wicked problems become inevitable if we solely use truth value as the golden standard to assess arts-based methods.

The alternative proposition is judging arts-based methods and the artworks produced on their aesthetic value. Here Gadamer's (2004) view on aesthetics can shed light on the purposes of arts-based research. According to Gadamer (2004), truth emerges from the experience of art and is not in contrast to reality. The purpose of arts-based research is not to seek fact but to provoke thought. To legitimise truth in the experience of art, researchers and research participants should first embrace a multiplicity of experiences and then allow artistic expressions (even though they might be incomplete, contradictory, or non-conceptual) to alter the being of the experiencer (Devereaux, 1991; Gadamer, 2004).

Taking drama as an example, comedies and tragedies have the power to bring hidden truth of life to light and transform both players and spectators during performances. Hence, Gadamer (2004) claimed that 'art supersedes reality, transforming it into its truth' (p. 11). Taking literary art as another example, Gadamer (2004) argued that it was not only futile but also problematic to aim to 'understand a writer better than he understood himself' (p. 19). Just as there are a thousand Hamlets in a thousand people's eyes, our understanding of a piece of literary art is context-mediated and subjective. Judging an artwork on its aesthetic value means we are not reducing the complex human world to one version of reality but embracing the multiple truths evoked by arts-based methods.

To sum up, this chapter examines the impact of arts-based research methods on research methodology enrichment, knowledge decolonisation, and policymaking. Knowledge produced in the academic realm has been continuously commodified. This further perpetuates the knowledge-based power imbalance between the privileged few and the marginalised groups. Research evidence shows that arts-based research methods can effectively break down barriers to access by empowering research participants to use creative tools that are familiar and friendly to them. Breaking down barriers also imposes risks. How to create a difference-attuned space of empathy that holds up personal boundaries in knowledge co-creation and emotion-intensive research processes is a key ethical issue for researchers to address. Lastly, this chapter has discussed another controversy surrounding arts-based research methods and artworks, which is whether to judge quality based on truth value or aesthetic value. Following in Gadamer's (2004) footsteps, I contend that good arts-based research should be thought-provoking; embracing a multiplicity of experiences is at its core.

References

Anyon, J. (2005). *Radical possibilities: Public policy, urban education, and a new social movement* (1st ed.). Routledge.

Boler, M. (1997). The risks of empathy: Interrogating multiculturalism's gaze. *Cultural Studies*, *11*(2), 253–273. https://doi.org/10.1080/09502389700490141

Boler, M. (1999). *Feeling power: Emotions and education* (1st ed.). Routledge.

Butler, J. (2004). *Undoing gender* (1st ed.). Routledge.

Calderon, E., Kustatscher, M., Tisdall, K., Evanko, T., & Gomez, J. M. (2022). Decolonising participatory methods with children and young people in international research collaborations: Reflections from a participatory arts-based project with Afrocolombian and indigenous young people in Colombia. In M. Moncrieffe (Ed.), *Decolonising curriculum knowledge: International perspectives & interdisciplinary approaches*. Palgrave Macmillan.

Chappell, S. V., & Cahnmann-Taylor, M. (2013). No child left with crayons: The imperative of arts-based education and research with language "minority" and other minoritized communities. *Review of Research in Education, 37*(1), 243–268. https://doi.org/10.3102/0091732X12461615

Cheng, S. (2004). *Law, justice, and power: Between reason and will*. Stanford University Press.

Daniels, D. (2002). Using the life histories of community builders in an informal settlement to advance the emancipation and development of women. In R. M. Cervero (Ed.), *The Cyril O. Houle scholars in adult and continuing education program global research* (Vol. 2, pp. 56–69). The University of Georgia. https://eric.ed.gov/?id=ED470937

Darder, A., Baltodano, M. P., & Torres, R. D. (Eds.). (2017). *The critical pedagogy reader* (3rd ed.). Routledge.

Datoo, A. K., & Chagani, Z. M. A. (2011). Street theatre: Critical pedagogy for social studies education. *Social Studies Research and Practice, 6*(2), 21–30. https://doi.org/10.1108/SSRP-02-2011-B0002

Devereaux, M. (1991). Can art save us?: A meditation on Gadamer. *Philosophy and Literature, 15*(1), 59–73. https://doi.org/10.1353/phl.1991.0056

Faulkner, S. L. (2019). *Poetic inquiry: Craft, method and practice* (2nd ed.). Routledge. https://doi.org/10.4324/9781351044233

Fitzpatrick, E., & Fitzpatrick, K. (2020). What poetry does for us in education and research. In E. Fitzpatrick & K. Fitzpatrick (Eds.), *Poetry, method and education research: Doing critical, decolonising and political inquiry*. Routledge.

Gadamer, H.-G. (2004). *Truth and method* (1st English ed.). Continuum.

Garakani, T. (2014). Young people have a lot to say . . . with trust, time, and tools: The voices of Inuit youth in Nunavik. *Canadian Journal of Education/Revue canadienne de l'éducation, 37*(1), 233–257.

Goodley, D., Liddiard, K., & Runswick-Cole, K. (2018). Feeling disability: Theories of affect and critical disability studies. *Disability & Society, 33*(2), 197–217. https://doi.org/10.1080/09687599.2017.1402752

Hammond, C., Gifford, W., Thomas, R., Rabaa, S., Thomas, O., & Domecq, M.-C. (2018). Arts-based research methods with indigenous peoples: An international scoping review. *AlterNative: An International Journal of Indigenous Peoples, 14*(3), 260–276. https://doi.org/10.1177/1177180118796870

Hope-Gill, L. (2020). The Munchkin and the medicine man: Poetry's place in a "hard" world. In E. Fitzpatrick & K. Fitzpatrick (Eds.), *Poetry, method and education research* (pp. 121–131). Routledge.

Myers, M., & Bhopal, K. (2021). Cosmopolitan brands: Graduate students navigating the social space of elite global universities. *British Journal of Sociology of Education, 42*(5–6), 701–716. https://doi.org/10.1080/01425692.2021.1941763

O'Neill, M., Erel, U., Kaptani, E., & Reynolds, T. (2019). Borders, risk and belonging: Challenges for arts-based research in understanding the lives of women asylum seekers and migrants "at the borders of humanity". *Crossings: Journal of Migration and Culture, 10*(1), 129–147. https://doi.org/10.1386/cjmc.10.1.129_1

Peters, M. A. (2015). Why is my curriculum white? *Educational Philosophy and Theory, 47*(7), 641–646. https://doi.org/10.1080/00131857.2015.1037227

Rice, C., Cook, K., & Bailey, K. A. (2021). Difference-attuned witnessing: Risks and potentialities of arts-based research. *Feminism & Psychology, 31*(3), 345–365. https://doi.org/10.1177/0959353520955142

Ruiz-Mallén, I., Heras, M., & Berrens, K. (2021). Responsible research and innovation in science education: Insights from evaluating the impact of using digital media and arts-based methods on RRI values. *Research in Science & Technological Education, 39*(3), 263–284. https://doi.org/10.1080/02635143.2020.1763289

Schultz, B. D. (2008). *Spectacular things happen along the way: Lessons from an urban classroom*. Teachers College Press.

Wilson, S. (2008). *Research is ceremony: Indigenous research methods*. Fernwood Publishing. https://eduq.info/xmlui/handle/11515/35872

Wyse, D., Brown, C., Oliver, S., & Poblete, X. (2017). *The BERA: Close-to-practice research project research report*. The British Educational Research Association.

Yuen, F., Linds, W., Goulet, L., Schmidt, K., Episkenew, J.-A., & Ritenburg, H. (2013). "You might as well call it planet of the Sioux": Indigenous youth, imagination, and decolonization. *Pimatisiwin, 11*(2), 269–282.

7 Future development and conclusion

Further theorising arts-based research methods

Over the past two decades, arts-based research has proliferated within the field of education. By July 2022, Taylor & Francis Group had published 5,354 books on arts-based research under the subject of education, of which 752 were about research methods, CPD, and study skills. Research centres, special interest groups (e.g. the American Educational Research Association and the British Educational Research Association), and educational conferences have attracted scholars who share similar research and methodological interests (Cahnmann-Taylor & Siegesmund, 2018). The popularity of arts-based research methods is also evidenced by the emergence of hybrid disciplines such as 'visual sociology, ethnographic performance, or poetic anthropology' (Cahnmann-Taylor & Siegesmund, 2018, p. 2). In addition to sociology and anthropology, educational research also widely uses arts-based inquiry.

In Chapter 6 of this book, I discussed how arts-based methods contribute to close-to-practice educational research, knowledge decolonisation, and education policymaking. Tracking the future development of arts-based research methods, I identified three lines of development work, namely further theorising arts-based research methods, incorporating artistic techniques into empirical studies, and using arts-based methods as a form of activism.

In terms of the theorisation of arts-based research, discussions on embodiment and aesthetics will continue to stimulate new research designs and methods. For example, scholars have revitalised Merleau-Ponty's phenomenology of embodiment to establish first person investigation into arts-based research in education (Nathan, 2021; Stolz & Thorburn, 2021; Thorburn & Stolz, 2020). Merleau-Ponty's (1983, 2013) concept of embodiment is particularly relevant to arts-based research, as he pointed out that the body was both a biological structure and a milieu that shaped the conscious mind,

DOI: 10.4324/9781003196105-7

cognition, and experience. Merleau-Ponty (1983) rejected the Cartesian dualism and its subsequent mind-body dichotomy. He argued that, as human beings, our physical movement helped us to better understand our being and relationship with the world. In the same vein, arts-based research focuses on human beings' embodied experience through artistic performance such as drama, dance, painting, and crafting. One direction for future development is to understand how bodily expression underpins arts-based research methodologies in education and how to utilise Merleau-Ponty's concept of embodiment to intertwine subjective experience and objective existence in educational research (Stolz & Thorburn, 2021).

In addition to embodiment, Gadamer's (2002) hermeneutical aesthetics is another concept that can assist scholars to advance arts-based research methods. Gadamer did not conceptualise aesthetics from the perspective of pleasure or beauty; instead, he emphasised that artwork itself can communicate its meaning and transform the viewer (Davey, 2013; Gjesdal, 2012). This relational and dialogical property of the arts resonates with the relational materialist ontology and anti-representationalism I presented in Chapter 2 of this book. To further theorise arts-based research methods, scholars may draw inspiration from Gadamer's aesthetics as a form of resistance against reductionism (Gadamer, 2002). Reasons why Gadamer's aesthetics can provide a new perspective to judge the value and purposes of arts-based methods are explained in Chapter 6.

Incorporating artistic techniques in empirical studies

The second line of development work is applying arts-based techniques in empirical studies. Arts-based research is a creative space. Modern digital technology has provided low-budget and sometimes open-source artistic applications and software to edit and manipulate photos, videos, and sound. Many of these digital tools are intuitive to use and thus lower the barriers to entry further for users. The European Commission (2012) strongly endorses digital technologies and artistic techniques as a means to promote responsible research and innovation (Ruiz-Mallén et al., 2021). Scholars have recognised that not just the arts but also disciplines such as science, technology, engineering, and mathematics all require students' mental effort, emotional engagement, affective motivation, and embodied experience (Woods-McConney et al., 2014).

The science–arts dichotomy is not only false but also harmful in education and in educational research. Incorporating arts-based techniques in empirical research has the potential to promote participants' affective motivation and engagement. Traditional research methods often employ pre- and post-intervention surveys as well as control and experiment groups to measure progress. One study showed that although students' cognitive understanding of the genetics concept in science education did not differ from their counterparts in the control group after playing a computer-based learning game, their motivation and interaction time with the learning environment had increased (Annetta et al., 2009). This finding has broadened the research scope from solely measuring cognitive achievement to accounting for affective motivation and its long-term impact on learning. One recommendation for educational researchers is to examine whether arts-based techniques can bring new perspectives, rather than supplementing the existing research tools.

Another study conducted in Hong Kong has found that arts-based methods such as 'open inquiry, problem-solving, creative writing, making metaphors and analogies, creating drama, rewriting songs, and inventing new products' can stimulate students' curiosity and self-satisfaction (Cheng, 2011, p. 72). Nevertheless, the Confucian culture in many Asian societies tends to devalue these playful methods unless the participants are convinced of their positive long-term effect on top of having short-term fun. This study reminds researchers to be aware of the cultural readiness for arts-based research methods when incorporating them into traditional research approaches.

Lastly, Rodrigues (2007) urges researchers to pay special attention to the role of symbolic representation when incorporating arts-based techniques into empirical studies. When using simulations in a study on students' learning of science, Rodrigues (2007) found that students' information processing skills may interfere with their learning capabilities. This means that students can rely on 'shared symbol identification' or the 'ability to discern the designers' logic of instructions' to falsely construct their knowledge on the subject (Rodrigues, 2007, p. 11). For example, some symbols (e.g. a key or the red–amber–green colour code) used in arts-based techniques may suggest particular meanings that eventually mislead participants. When discussing how to choose materials for arts-based research in Chapter 3 of this book, I pointed out that research participants may assign certain meaning to some symbols that are relevant in their particular socio-cultural contexts. For future research, scholars should make explicit how art materials used in research may cause cognitive confusion and mitigate this risk.

Using arts-based methods as a form of activism

Many examples of the research projects I have presented in previous chapters highlight the power of arts-based research as a form of activism. Decolonising methodologies is an indispensable part of decolonising knowledge

Future development and conclusion 65

because methodologies determine how knowledge is acquired. Arts-based inquiry creates a space of contention between people and politics as well as between the privileged and the marginalised groups to negotiate, conflict, coalesce, and collaborate in the meaning-making process (Knowles & Cole, 2008). Following this line of argument, one can further contend that arts-based methods carry the mission of transforming existing social, cultural, and political structures and power relations, and they therefore can be seen as a form of activism.

Keifer-Boyd (2011) connects arts-based research with feminist activism because it '(a) responsibly listens to subalterns' voices and entangled histories; (b) bears witness and reveals power structures that control people, cultural narratives, and hegemonic worldviews; (c) stops traffic of harmful activities and products; and (d) envisions' (p. 3). Not just for fighting against gender inequality, arts-based methods address different types of exclusion and inequality. Using Gramsci's concept of subaltern, De Kock (1992) defined subalterns as people who 'do not have access to participation in the hegemonic discourse to speak of their oppression or space of difference' (Keifer-Boyd, 2011, p. 4). Fricker (2007) coined the term hermeneutical injustice to describe failing to understand or articulate a harmful experience due to a lack of hermeneutical resources such as vocabulary and concepts. The root cause of hermeneutical injustice is marginalised individuals or groups lacking access to collective hermeneutical resources or being rejected to participate in knowledge creation. Research is a knowledge-intensive activity. Most traditional research methods tend to assign researchers a powerful status because they hold powerful knowledge featuring rationalist thinking (Carlgren, 2020; Hordern, 2022; Young & Muller, 2013). Research participants, especially subalterns who lack access to collective hermeneutical resources, are in an inferior position. They struggle to make their lived experiences intelligible to researchers who, more often than not, do not share the same epistemic background (Fricker, 2007, 2017; Tian & Nutbrown, 2021). Arts-based methods, as I introduced in Chapters 1, 2, and 6, are committed to transforming this knowledge–power imbalance and giving research participants an equal epistemic status as knowers.

To date, scholars who have theorised and developed arts-based research methods have recognised a wide spectrum of epistemic resources, including body language, feelings, and artefacts (Butler-Kisber, 2010). Through artmaking, research participants are empowered to re-imagine reality and to challenge existing sociocultural structures (Eaves, 2014; Keifer-Boyd, 2011). The next stage of development calls for actions leading to change. Arts-based methods create a space for contention, as I illustrated earlier. They also create a safe space for subalterns to build confidence by using their cultural capital. One study has shown that, because of their vulnerable social status, migrants tend to adopt a passive approach in social life; however, by engaging with arts-based research projects, their artistic abilities and self-belief grow over time (Rydzik et al., 2013). This form of empowerment has the potential to transform them into activists who can voice their differences in political, social, and cultural discourses. Following empowerment, it is positive change that educational researchers and research participants aim to bring through arts-based methods.

Conclusion

Thanks to the great effort made by scholars over the past decades, arts-based research methods are no longer seen as a 'monkey business' (Grumet, 2017, p. 12), and there is increasing recognition of their ability to empower research participants to co-create knowledge with the researcher (Ball et al., 2021; Eaves, 2014; Rydzik et al., 2013). By doing so, arts-based methods enable us to see a new way of conducting research that is performative, non-linear, and non-reductionist.

In Chapter 1 of this book, I lay the groundwork for arts-based research methods in education. I argue that the purpose of engaging with creative techniques is not to represent or relive the reality but rather to re-imagine it. The reductionist approach in research tends to distil knowledge to the extent that much nuanced meaning and context is lost. Consequently, research findings are becoming increasingly detached from real social problems and the people of concern. Our over-reliance on linguistic resources in research (e.g. conducting interviews and document analysis) appears to alienate research participants who have limited access to collective epistemic resources. Many research participants may not have a large arsenal of vocabulary and sophisticated concepts to make their lived experiences intelligible during a 45-minute interview. How to effectively tap into their knowledge is a question for researchers who embrace arts-based research methods to answer. Researchers have found that artefacts have the power to elicit and convey feelings when language fails (Woods & Roberts, 2016). The intra-action of language, the body, material, and environment give meaning to our being and relationship with the world (Barad, 2003, 2007). Hence, research should not be reduced to using language as the only form of communication.

In Chapter 2, I proposed my ontological, epistemological, and axiological stances when designing and conducting arts-based research in education. Although they do not provide the only right answers to the big questions of what arts-based research is and how we should conduct it, they offer readers some examples and help them to establish their own positionalities as researchers. What I want to reiterate here is that the core of arts-based research methods is about empowerment, connection, and transformation.

Future development and conclusion 67

That requires researchers to revisit the concept of knowledge (i.e. epistemology) and the mechanism through which knowledge is acquired (i.e. methodology). Sharing an equal epistemic status between the researcher and the research participants is easier said than done. Delicate issues such as holding up ethical and emotional boundaries to allow authentic dialogues and empathy to flow without collapsing the sense of self should be carefully handled throughout the entire research process (see also Chapter 6).

There have been myriad methodology books introducing different designs of arts-based methods (Ball et al., 2021; Cahnmann-Taylor & Siegesmund, 2018; Foster, 2015; Jagodzinski & Wallin, 2013; Knowles & Cole, 2008). The purpose of this book is not to reinvent the wheel but to present some of my hands-on experience of how to use this methodology. Chapters 3, 4, and 5 use collage-making as an example to illustrate the research preparation, data collection, analysis, and reporting process. It is worth highlighting here that my research design, the materials used, and the techniques applied do not provide a blueprint for other research projects. I encourage readers to use my project as an example rather than an exemplar. As any other study, my research project has its limitations. Applying arts-based methods in educational research is not entirely like navigating uncharted waters but it does often push us out of our comfort zone. Sitting comfortably with uncertainties, embracing multiple viewpoints, and giving up control over a perfectly orchestrated research process are some lessons to learn for researchers.

Chapter 6 discusses the impact of arts-based research methods and some controversies surrounding them. Much evidence has shown that arts-based methods can profoundly impact close-to-practice research, knowledge decolonisation, and education policymaking by making tools of inquiry and research findings more accessible to the public. On the question of how to engage participants in arts-based research, scholars have debated the extent to which empathy facilitates trust building and when it affects participants' emotional wellbeing. I suggest having an open discussion with the participants on research ethics and agreeing on general principles within the group. Another controversy surrounding arts-based methods is how to assess the value of a project and its output. Scholars tend to agree that arts-based research is less about seeking infallible truth and more about evoking new perspectives and understandings that are rooted in reality.

In the final chapter of the book, I envisioned three lines of development for arts-based research. The concepts of embodiment and aesthetics can assist researchers to further theorise arts-based research methods. New technologies have lowered the cost and capacity barriers for researchers and participants to incorporate artistic techniques into research. Data can be presented in creative formats, such as in pictures, videos, audio, and performance arts. Because of the power of transformation, arts-based research methods have the potential to promote activism. So far, scholars have been focusing on using arts-based research to *speak for* marginalised and disadvantaged groups. The next step will be to use it to *act on* social changes.

Lastly, I would like to quote Hannah Arendt's (2017) words on how human beings understand and connect to the world. She wrote:

> Comprehension does not mean denying the outrageous, deducing the unprecedented from precedents, or explaining phenomena by such analogies and generalities that the impact of reality and the shock of experience are no longer felt. It means, rather, examining and bearing consciously the burden which our century has placed on us-neither denying its existence nor submitting meekly to its weight.
>
> (p. x)

The old reductionist and rationalist views on the world are no longer sufficient. To fully connect to reality, we need to embody experiences and feelings and at the same time defend our subjectivity within the larger social, cultural, and political structures. Whether you are an early-career researcher or an established scholar, I believe that everyone can feel the power of the arts and find meaning through their lenses. I hope you have found this book useful in the quest for educational research.

References

Annetta, L. A., Minogue, J., Holmes, S. Y., & Cheng, M.-T. (2009). Investigating the impact of video games on high school students' engagement and learning about genetics. *Computers & Education*, 53(1), 74–85. https://doi.org/10.1016/j.compedu.2008.12.020

Arendt, H. (2017). *The origins of totalitarianism* (18th ed.). Penguin Classics.

Ball, S., Leach, B., Bousfield, J., Smith, P., & Marjanovic, S. (2021). *Arts-based approaches to public engagement with research: Lessons from a rapid review* (p. 111). RAND Corporation.

Barad, K. (2003). Posthumanist performativity: Toward an understanding of how matter comes to matter. *Signs: Journal of Women in Culture and Society*, 28(3), 801–831. https://doi.org/10.1086/345321

Barad, K. (2007). *Meeting the universe halfway: Quantum physics and the entanglement of matter and meaning* (Illustrated ed.). Duke University Press.

Butler-Kisber, L. (2010). *Qualitative inquiry: Thematic, narrative and arts-informed perspectives*. SAGE.

Cahnmann-Taylor, M., & Siegesmund, R. (2018). *Arts-based research in education: Foundations for practice* (2nd ed.). Routledge.

Carlgren, I. (2020). Powerful knowns and powerful knowings. *Journal of Curriculum Studies*, 52(3), 323–336. https://doi.org/10.1080/00220272.2020.1717634

Cheng, V. M. Y. (2011). Infusing creativity into Eastern classrooms: Evaluations from student perspectives. *Thinking Skills and Creativity*, *6*(1), 67–87. https://doi.org/10.1016/j.tsc.2010.05.001

Davey, N. (2013). *Unfinished worlds: Hermeneutics, aesthetics and Gadamer* (1st ed.). Edinburgh University Press.

de Kock, L. (1992). An interview with Gayatri Chakravorty Spivak. *ARIEL: A Review of International English Literature*, *23*(3), 29–47.

Eaves, S. (2014). From art for art's sake to art as means of knowing: A rationale for advancing arts-based methods in research, practice and pedagogy. *Electronic Journal of Business Research Methods*, *12*(2), 154–167.

European Commission. (2012). *Research and innovation*. https://ec.europa.eu/info/research-and-innovation_en

Foster, V. (2015). *Collaborative arts-based research for social justice*. Routledge.

Fricker, M. (2007). *Epistemic injustice: Power and the ethics of knowing*. Oxford University Press. www.oxfordscholarship.com/view/10.1093/acprof:oso/9780198237907.001.0001/acprof-9780198237907

Fricker, M. (2017). Evolving concepts of epistemic injustice. In J. Kidd, J. Medina, & G. Pohlhaus Jr. (Eds.), *The Routledge handbook of epistemic injustice* (pp. 53–60). Routledge. https://doi.org/10.4324/9781315212043-5

Gadamer, H. (2002). *Gadamer in conversation: Reflections and commentary* (1st ed.). Yale University Press.

Gjesdal, K. (2012). *Gadamer and the legacy of German idealism*. Cambridge University Press.

Grumet, M. (2017). Celebrating monkey business in art education and research. In M. Cahnmann-Taylor & R. Siegesmund (Eds.), *Arts-based research in education: Foundations for practice* (2nd ed., pp. 12–18). Routledge. https://doi.org/10.4324/9781315305073-2

Hordern, J. (2022). Powerful knowledge and knowledgeable practice. *Journal of Curriculum Studies*, *54*(2), 196–209. https://doi.org/10.1080/00220272.2021.1933193

Jagodzinski, J., & Wallin, J. (2013). Arts-based research: A critique and a proposal. In *Arts-based research*. Brill Sense. https://brill.com/view/title/36660

Keifer-Boyd, K. (2011). Arts-based research as social justice activism: Insight, inquiry, imagination, embodiment, relationality. *International Review of Qualitative Research*, *4*(1), 3–19. https://doi.org/10.1525/irqr.2011.4.1.3

Knowles, J. G., & Cole, A. L. (2008). *Handbook of the arts in qualitative research: Perspectives, methodologies, examples, and issues*. SAGE.

Merleau-Ponty, M. (1983). *The structure of behavior* (1st English ed.). Duquesne University Press.

Merleau-Ponty, M. (2013). *Phenomenology of perception* (1st ed.). Routledge.

Nathan, M. J. (2021). *Foundations of embodied learning: A paradigm for education* (1st ed.). Routledge.

Rodrigues, S. (2007). Factors that influence pupil engagement with science simulations: The role of distraction, vividness, logic, instruction and prior knowledge. *Chemistry Education Research and Practice*, *8*(1), 1–12. https://doi.org/10.1039/B6RP90016J

Ruiz-Mallén, I., Heras, M., & Berrens, K. (2021). Responsible research and innovation in science education: Insights from evaluating the impact of using digital media and arts-based methods on RRI values. *Research in Science & Technological Education, 39*(3), 263–284. https://doi.org/10.1080/02635143.2020.1763289

Rydzik, A., Pritchard, A., Morgan, N., & Sedgley, D. (2013). The potential of arts-based transformative research. *Annals of Tourism Research, 40*, 283–305. https://doi.org/10.1016/j.annals.2012.09.006

Stolz, S. A., & Thorburn, M. (2021). Phenomenology, embodiment, and education: First-person methodologies of embodied subjectivity. In S. A. Stolz (Ed.), *The body, embodiment, and education* (pp. 60–78). Routledge. https://doi.org/10.4324/9781003142010-4

Thorburn, M., & Stolz, S. A. (2020). Understanding experience better in educational contexts: The phenomenology of embodied subjectivity. *Cambridge Journal of Education, 50*(1), 95–105. https://doi.org/10.1080/0305764X.2019.1632798

Tian, M., & Nutbrown, G. (2021). Retheorising distributed leadership through epistemic injustice. *Educational Management Administration & Leadership*, 17411432211022776. https://doi.org/10.1177/17411432211022776

Woods, P. A., & Roberts, A. (2016). Distributed leadership and social justice: Images and meanings from across the school landscape. *International Journal of Leadership in Education, 19*(2), 138–156. https://doi.org/10.1080/13603124.2015.1034185

Woods-McConney, A., Oliver, M. C., McConney, A., Schibeci, R., & Maor, D. (2014). Science engagement and literacy: A retrospective analysis for students in Canada and Australia. *International Journal of Science Education, 36*(10), 1588–1608. https://doi.org/10.1080/09500693.2013.871658

Young, M., & Muller, J. (2013). On the powers of powerful knowledge. *Review of Education, 1*(3), 229–250. https://doi.org/10.1002/rev3.3017

Index

Note: Page numbers in *italics* indicate a figure and page numbers in **bold** indicate a table on the corresponding page.

action research design 35
activism: arts-based methods as form of 5, 14, 52, 62, 64–65, 68
aesthetic and epistemic concerns, dialectic between 55
aesthetic awareness 35
aesthetics 21, 23; embodiment and 62, 67; hermeneutical 63
aesthetic value versus truth value 58–59
aesthetic reflexivity 35
affective attributes 35
affective containment 7
affective motivation 63
Afro-Colombia young people as subject group 56
analogies 64, 68
anthropocentrism 13
anthropology 62
anti-representationalism 63
Arendt, Hannah 68
Armstrong, John xvii
art(s): Aboriginal term for, lack of 3; explorative nature of 33; lived reality as represented by 4; as mode of enquiry 3; as tool of exploration 1; truth in the experience of 58; as vehicle of enquiry 14; *see also* artwork
art creation as shared encounter 17
art creation process 17, 30, 33; agency in 16

artefacts: capacity to convey meaning 66; choosing 25 (box), 46, **47**; in collage 48, 50; as epistemic resource 65; gold-plated PhD sword 1, *2*; non-human 7, 24
art-making process as meaning-making process 4–5, 14, 25; meta questions attached to 17
art materials: symbolic meanings of 15–16
arts and research 1–3
arts-based inquiry: spaces of contention created by 65
arts-based methods: critical reflection simulated by 56; historical and systemic oppressions capable of being challenged by 56; judging artworks based on truth value or aesthetic value 58–59; as inductive methodology 51
arts-based research in education: aesthetic tools used by 4; as creative space 63; criteria for assessing rigour of 32–35; data collection 32–44; empowerment, connection and transformation via 66; ethical considerations 7, 26–30; feminist activism and 65; increasing popularity of 26; interest in 4; lived realities challenged by 6; multiple modes of expression embraced/ employed by 3, 5; non-scientific

nature of 32; performatism[MT(E1] and performativity in 4–6; perpetuating provoking by 33; representationalism in 4–6; research design for 20–21; research rigour, assessing 32–44, 58; social sciences and 2; theorisation of 4; three lines of development for 62, 67–68
arts-based research methods: affective containment and 7; controversies surrounding 57–59, 67; decolonising knowledge via 55–56; educational leadership study using 6; embodiment and aesthetics in 67; emotional distress and 7; informing or changing educational policy via 56–57; as means of transformation 51; performativity, psychodynamics, materiality, and embodiment brought together by 8; post-humanist paradigm used to theorise 24
arts-based techniques: incorporating into empirical studies 64
artwork: aesthetic value of 58, 59; Armstrong on xvii; in arts-based educational research 35; co-creation of 33; de Botton on xvii; Gadamer on 63; informed consent related to 28–29; originality and creativity in xviii; student-made 23–25, 30; time required to create 17; truth value of 58; used to verify truthfulness 32
artwork-stimulated narration 25
artography 20
autoethnography 20
Austin, J. 5
Australia 3
authenticity and authentication 34, 48, 67
axiological assumptions 11
axiology 3, 66; definition of 12, 15; epistemic quality and 15–18; procedural ethics of 15; relational ethics of 15

Baldwin, J. 33
balloons 23, 30, **40–41**, 48
Barad, K. 4, 5, 8; intra-action 8, 13
Barone, T. 32, 33, 34
Benner, P. 8
Bion, Wilfred 7

body language 65
body, the 8, 11, 13, 21, 66; Merleau-Ponty on 62–63; mind–body dichotomy 8, 63
Boler, M. 57
Botton, Alain de xvii
Bourriaud, N. 17
British Educational Research Association (BERA) 12, 26, 54, 62
Brockelman, T. 21
Butler, J. 5, 57
Butler-Kisber, L. 21

Calderon, E. 56
Canada 3; Inuit people of 56
Carter, B., and Ford, K. 30
ceremony 3; university conferment (*promootio*, Finnish) 1
Cartesian dualism 63
Chawla-Duggan, R. 33
child-friendly approaches 30
childhood education, early 4
children and young people in arts-based research 29–31; Afro-Colombian and indigenous 56; digital cameras given to 33; father-child interaction 33; special needs 12
China *see* distributed leadership in Finnish and Chinese schools
Confucianism 64
collage and collage-making 21; consent for workshop involving 28–29 box); distributed leadership in Finnish and Chinese schools, project on 36–44; examples of **37–42**; follow-up interview questions after, examples of 25–26 (box); formative findings based in **47**; reporting and discussing findings 46–52
collage made by LC1 *40*, 46
collage made by LF1 *37*, 46, 47, 49
collage made by TC1 *41*, 46, 47, 48, 49
collage made by TF1 *38*, 46, 47
collage workshop preparation questions, examples of 21–22
comparability 4
consensual validation 34
contention, spaces of 65
copyright 30; informed consent form question regarding 29 (box)

critical realism 12, 13–15
curriculum decolonisation movement, UK 55
curriculum reform 6

Dakota First Nation 56
Dale, D. and James, C. 6, 7
decolonisation and identity 56
decolonisation movement *see* curriculum decolonisation movement, UK
decolonising knowledge 55–56, 57, 59, 62, 64–65; *see also* knowledge
De Kock, L. 65
Denzin, N. 51
derivative work 30
dialectical reflexivity 33
disabled/nondisabled 57
disadvantaged communities 55, 68
distributed leadership: nonteaching staff understudied in research about 51; resource-agency duality model of *43*, 49; uncovering what it is/can be 52
distributed leadership in Finnish and Chinese schools 4, 22, 25, 43; informed consent form, example of 28–29 (box); project on 36–44, 46; reporting and discussing findings on project 46–52, 67; *see also* European Arts-Based Development of Distributed Leadership and Innovation in Schools (ENABLES)
distributed leadership knowledge 51
Donati, P. 13
drawings xv; 2D 1; facilitated 56

Eco, Umberto xiv
educational research 1–9; collage making for 21; embodiment in 8; preparation 21–24; psychodynamics in 6–7
educational leadership knowledge, awareness, and capabilities 35
educational leadership study: arts-based research methods used for 6
educational researchers: axiological issues to be considered by 12; entanglement issues to be considered by 13, 14; epistemologies useful to 12; ethical issues important to 12; methodological questions to be addressed in research design 11–12; stances taken by 9
Egyptian hieroglyphs 1
Eisner, E. 4, 34
Ellingson, L. 8
embodied experience 33, 63; materiality and 7–9
embodied knowledge 36
embodied learning process 35
embodied meaning 17
embodied processing of scientific content 56
embodiment 8, 67; Merleau-Ponty's concept of 62–64
emotional distress 15
emotional engagement 63
emotionally safe environment 30, 44
emotional safe space 17, 54
emotional wellbeing 7, 12, 58, 67
empathy 7, 57–58, 67; difference-attuned 58, 59
ENABLES project *see* European Arts-Based Development of Distributed Leadership and Innovation in Schools
Enlightenment, the xiv, 2–3, 55
entangled histories 65
entanglement 8, 13–14, 24
ethical considerations in arts-based research 7, 26–30; *see also* informed consent; procedural ethics
Ethical Guidelines for Educational Research (BERA) 12
ethical guidelines *see* ethical considerations in arts-based research
ethnocinema 20
ethnodrama 20
ethnographic performance 62
ethnotheatre 20
European Arts-Based Development of Distributed Leadership and Innovation in Schools (ENABLES project) 35, 45
European Commission 56, 63

Faulkner, S. 55
feelings 3; artefacts' ability to convey 66; arts-based research capacity to tap into and externalise 7, 16, 18, 25; collage's ability to evoke 21,

23, 24, 28; empathy and 57; logic of naturalist inquiry in relationship to 51; negative 6; positive 6; research designed to evoke 33, 34; sharing 44
feminine leadership 41
feminism 2, 12
feminist activism: arts-based research and 65
Finland 1; *see also* distributed leadership in Finnish and Chinese schools
Fricker, M. 65

Gadamer H. -G. 58–59, 62–63
gender 5, 36
gender equality 56, 57
gender inequality 65
Goodley, D. 57
Goya, Francisco xvii
Gramsci, A. 65

Hammond, C. 56
Harman, R. and Zhang, X. 6
hermeneutical aesthetics 63
hermeneutical injustice 65
Hong Kong 62
Hope-Gill, L. 55
Husserl, E. 13

informed consent 12, 26
informed consent form 22, 28, 36, 44; example of 28–29 (box)
intersubjective arts-space 46
intersubjective relations 46
intra-action 8, 13, 15, 16, 18, 21, 66
Inuit people of Canada 56

James, C. 6, 7
Jia-Gu-Wen 1

Keifer-Boyd, K. 65
knowers 17, 65
knowledge: co-creation of 17, 18, 58, 66; cognitive embodied 36; decolonising 55–56, 57, 59, 62, 64–65; objective 2; reducing uncertainty using 32; in relational materialist ontology 13; transitive nature of 14; *see also* axiology; epistemology
knowledge base 50

knowledge contributors 25
knowledge creation 65
knowledge politics 55
knowledge position 15, 17, 18
knowledge production 8, 14; neoliberal 55

language: Aboriginal 3; ancient 1; arts-based research methods and 11; intra-action of body, material, environment and 8, 13, 21, 66; organised 7; performative 5; power of 6, 24; slow-paced (child friendly) 30; rational thinking and 2
language-based reasoning 24
language of science 55
learning: collaborative 35; embodied 35
learning by doing 8
learning game, computer-based 64
"learning" in the real world 14
Leavy, P. 20
literacy 20
lived experiences: collage-making as representation of 23–25, 36, 46, 50; empathising with another's lived experiences 58; entanglement of 8; knowers, different lived experiences of 17; knowledge production as 8; making lived experiences intelligible to others 66; making sense of 26; perceptional representations of 5; recalling and retelling 4; reporting on/articulating xvii–xviii; research process as meaning-making processed tied to 32; risk of decontextualising 58; of school leadership, as represented through artwork (collage) 36, 46, 50; street theatre method used to express 54; struggle of subalterns to express 65; truth according to 58; understanding another's lived experiences 57
lived experiences and feelings: unintelligible or subconscious 25
lived realities: arts-based research and 6
Locke, John xiv

Marshall, Chrissiejoy 3
materiality 7–9, 24
Mayer, R. 32, 34

McNiff, S. 14
Merleau-Ponty, M. 62–63
metaphors 33, 64
meta questions 17
migrants and immigrants 54, 61, 66
mind–body dichotomy 8, 63
Museo del Prado xvii

narrative inquiry 20; *see also* visual-narrative inquiry 24–26
narratives 13, 24, 43, 44, 46, 48, 49; cultural 65; reclaiming 55
naturalistic inquiry, logic of 51
natural reality 14
nature, classification of xv
nature of ethics *see* axiology
nature of knowledge 11, 14
Norris, J. 30

ontology 3, 11; *see also* relational materialism/relational materialist ontology
oppressed minorities 54
oppression, cultures of 57, 65

performance 5; artistic 63; ethnographic 62
performative arts 20, 67
performativism 4–7, 32, 66
performativity 5, 6, 8
performative language 5
phenomena 4, 5, 22 (box), 32; complex 52; educational xviii, 7, 21, 33; explaining 68; interpretations of 32, 34; social 2, 14, 51; studied 22 (box) 24; understanding of 25, 34, 35
phenomenological ontology 13
phenomenology 5, 62
post-humanism 2, 12; Taylor and Gannon on 20
post-humanist approach 7, 8
post-humanist paradigm 24
post-structuralism 2
pragmatism 12, 55
procedural ethics 15, 26, 29
psychodynamics 6–7

qualitative approaches 5
qualitative inquiry 21

qualitative interview 4
qualitative research and methods 3, 8, 13, 15, 32
quantitative surveys 4, 35

racial inequality 55, 57
reciprocal 36
relational 36
relational capabilities 35
relational ethics 15, 17–18
relational good 58
relational leadership 51
relational materialism/relational materialist ontology 12–14, 63
relationships as reality 3
reliability 4
resource-agency duality model of distributed leadership *43*, 49
Rice, C. 57, 58
Rodrigues, S. 62

safe space 17
Siegesmund, R. 33
social injustice and power abuse 49, 55, 57–58; *see also* hermeneutical injustice
social reality/social relationality 13
Somerville, M. 3
subaltern, the 65

Taylor, C. and Gannon, S. 20
Tian, Meng 43
transferability 4

validity 4
Verlie, B. 13
video games 56
video recording 16, 16, 46, 63, 67
visual-narrative inquiry 22, 24–26
visual reflexivity 33

watercolours 15
White curriculum 55
White scholars 55
Wilson, S. 3
Woods, P. 36, 50

young people *see* children and young people in arts-based research

Taylor & Francis eBooks

www.taylorfrancis.com

A single destination for eBooks from Taylor & Francis with increased functionality and an improved user experience to meet the needs of our customers.

90,000+ eBooks of award-winning academic content in Humanities, Social Science, Science, Technology, Engineering, and Medical written by a global network of editors and authors.

TAYLOR & FRANCIS EBOOKS OFFERS:

- A streamlined experience for our library customers
- A single point of discovery for all of our eBook content
- Improved search and discovery of content at both book and chapter level

REQUEST A FREE TRIAL
support@taylorfrancis.com

For Product Safety Concerns and Information please contact our EU representative GPSR@taylorandfrancis.com
Taylor & Francis Verlag GmbH, Kaufingerstraße 24, 80331 München, Germany

www.ingramcontent.com/pod-product-compliance
Lightning Source LLC
Chambersburg PA
CBHW070601170426
43201CB00012B/1898